SUSHI MASTER

An expert guide to sourcing, making, and enjoying sushi at home

NICK SAKAGAMI

TOYOSU (TSUKIJI) CERTIFIED
OSAKANA (FISH) MEISTER #109

chartwell
books

Quarto

This edition published in 2023 by Chartwell Books,
an imprint of The Quarto Group
142 West 36th Street, 4th Floor
New York, NY 10018 USA
T (212) 779-4972 F (212) 779-6058
www.Quarto.com

First Published in 2019 by Quarry Books,
an imprint of The Quarto Group,
100 Cummings Center, Suite 265-D,
Beverly, MA 01915, USA.
T (978) 282-9590 F (978) 283-2742

Chartwell Books titles are also available at discount for retail, wholesale, promotional, and bulk
purchase. For details, contact the Special Sales Manager by email at specialsales@quarto.com or by
mail at The Quarto Group, Attn: Special Sales Manager, 100 Cummings Center, Suite 265-D, Beverly,
MA 01915, USA.

10 9 8 7 6 5 4 3 2 1

ISBN: 978-0-7858-4309-2

Interior Design and page layout: Timothy Samara
Cover Design: Michael Caputo
Cover photo: Shutterstock
Photography: Kristin Teig except endpapers and pages 7, 10, 17, 21, 23–29, 32, 34, 35,
43, 52, 56, 58, 65, 69 are by Laia Albaladejo

Printed in China

To my father,
who loved the ocean.
He left for another voyage
before seeing this book.

CONTENTS

My introduction to fish started when I was young—my father often took me fishing. In my twenties, I worked for a seafood wholesaler. I smelled like fish. I dreamt about fish. I would become excited just being around fish. This is why, over the years, I've taken the time to continue my education about fish and become the *only person* outside Japan to be certified as an *osakana meister*—a fish master.

Today my life is still all about fish. I wake up very early in the morning, on West Coast time in Los Angeles, and get on the phone with East Coast buyers and wholesalers. I work to import fresh tuna from Tahiti, collaborating with local families and the fishing industry there. Then I deal with West Coast buyers, meeting with wholesalers and restaurants to educate them about fresh fish and sustainable practices. Often I do consulting gigs, traveling to San Francisco, Chicago, and New York. I want the world to experience food made from the freshest fish, and I want that experience to be sustainable and possible without too much difficulty or cost.

In this book, you will discover information that only fish wholesalers know. You will learn tips and techniques some people in the seafood industry might not be happy about sharing, such as the best methods for selecting and sourcing fish, the truth about "bright pink colored" tuna and certain fishing methods, plus how to properly cut fish for your sashimi, from a loin to a block to sashimi pieces, and more. And, by following my advice on how to find sustainably caught fish, you help support the many hardworking, honest, and responsible people working in the seafood industry.

This book is about making sushi at home. When you make it at home, you incur less expense than buying it at a restaurant. As you start making sushi yourself, you will gain an understanding of how detailed the process can be and why the process is as important as the product. This will also offer you a new understanding of what professional sushi chefs do. Another positive outcome of making your own sushi at home: You can eat like a pig and drink like a skunk and not have to drive at the end of the evening. (It's always recommended to pair your food with the local alcoholic beverage, and, in this case, that's sake, of course.) This book also covers the correct ways to eat sushi, so the experience is enjoyed to its fullest.

Because sushi is so very simple, what goes inside—the tiny details—are most important. While I treasure and respect the artistic creations by the master chefs, the basics are attainable and not a big deal. Well, not a big deal when you know how to pick the right fish, slice the fish, and make the basic components of sushi dishes.

Once you learn the basics, there are some advanced techniques if you are curious to learn more. And throughout the book, my dear chef-friends share recipes to bring the whole experience up a notch or two for you.

I also want to introduce how we, the consumers, can play a small, yet important, part in ensuring future generations have fresh fish, so I talk about sustainable fishing practices throughout the book. Seafood consumption is on the rise, globally. The world population is expected to grow. How do we ensure there will always be plenty of fish in the sea?

One book is not enough to cover this complicated and always evolving subject fully. Yet, once you know the basics, you can build upon your knowledge. Different fish, different techniques . . . I hope this will be a gateway to a new chapter of your culinary journey.

Now, let's roll!

*The author enjoying a fresh bite at the
Tsukiji Fish Market in Tokyo, Japan*

What Is Sushi?

Chutoro, medium-marbled belly of ranched bluefin tuna (top). Otoro, ravishly marbled belly of ranched bluefin tuna.

At its most basic, *sushi*, which means, "sour tasting" in Japanese, is vinegared rice with various toppings. Its origins go back centuries: Salted fish packed in rice was fermented as a way of preserving it. Contemporary sushi, vinegared rice topped with fish, what we know as *nigiri sushi*, was created as a finger food for the construction workers in Tokyo back in the early 1600s. In need of nutritious food that could be eaten quickly, the workers found this to be the perfect solution. Sushi was a fast food, usually consumed while standing.

SUSHI TODAY

While nigiri was the original form of sushi, today sushi takes many forms. The basic forms are:

———

Chirashizushi A bowl of sushi ingredients scattered on top of rice

———

Maki Rolls made with vinegared rice and various ingredients rolled within sheets of nori (seaweed); outside Japan, this is sometimes made with the rice on the outside, like an inside-out roll.

———

Nigiri Slices of fish on vinegared rice, usually with wasabi

———

Sashimi A slice of fish that is consumed raw without rice. If you use low-quality fish, it will clearly show. Sashimi is also friendly for low-carb diets, as there is almost no carbs yet tons of high-quality protein in good fish.

———

Temaki Hand rolls made with sushi ingredients and rice wrapped with a sheet of nori, shaped into a cone

Another way sushi has evolved is with regard to the kinds of fish that are popular. Before refrigeration, sushi was made with preserved fish and fish that kept well. *Toro*, tuna belly, wasn't used for sushi because oily fish didn't keep well. Salmon was not a sushi fish in Japan until about twenty years ago. Now it is one of the top sellers in both Japan and the United States.

Sushi is now available all over the world and in all kinds of places. You can find sushi at grocery stores, fast-food places, and high-end restaurants, where it continues to evolve.

While traditional sushi in Japan is very simple and usually doesn't contain more than one type of fish or vegetable, American-style sushi is more elaborate. Spicy mayonnaise used in sushi is an example of how sushi is evolving. Where Japanese sushi is a delicate balance of flavors, Western diners prefer bold flavors and strong colors, which explains the popularity of a roll such as the Philadelphia roll, which includes salmon, avocado, and cream cheese.

CULTURE AND PHILOSOPHY

Most anyone can create sushi by making a simple rice ball and putting a piece of fish over it. But when sushi is made by a master, it becomes an art form where less is more.

Sushi represents a culture that strives toward perfectionism—one that sees mastery in the art of simplicity. Great purity follows from simplicity; hence, the finest sushi is simple in appearance. A passion for perfection drives the sushi chef to apply exacting standards of freshness and a perfect balance of flavors and textures.

By making your own sushi, you gain a deeper understanding of Japanese culture. Sushi making requires flexibility and adaptability, characteristics of Japanese people. Japan is a small country, but it stretches north almost to Siberia where people go to ski and in the other direction to tropical climates. In Japan people must deal with hurricanes, typhoons, snow, and now tornadoes. They have to be flexible to coexist with nature in its many forms. While other parts of the world try to control nature, the Japanese try to respect what nature brings and live with it. The Japanese may trim their natural surroundings and do small things to maintain it, but they try to let nature and people coexist in harmony.

I'm so happy that sushi is popular worldwide. Sushi can solve many problems in the world. It's healthful to eat; good health makes people happy, which leads to a more peaceful world. The more we find ourselves stuck behind an electronic screen, the more we want to reach out and reset the mind and find Zen and contemplation. Just like the Zen garden, with sushi, you trim away unnecessary things and enjoy what's left—you don't add. In search of simplicity, people are finding new appreciation of the simple nigiri. It takes true knowledge to understand simplicity. Nigiri is clean and simple—the vinegar, the texture of the rice, the knife work; they are all appreciated when you take the time to savor it.

An antidote to our hectic lives and often-artificial surroundings, sushi is welcome simplicity. Sushi lets you go deeper and deeper into sourcing fresh ingredients, absent artificial preservatives. All you need are time and resources to bring fresh ingredients to your table.

Mastery of the form doesn't happen overnight. It takes knowledge and practice to achieve the pure simplicity behind making sushi.

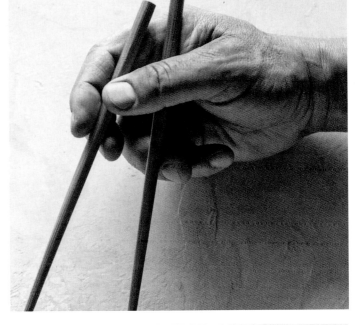

Holding hashi correctly

SUSHI ETIQUETTE

As with all traditional dining, there are rules and manners. In the West, for example, as you dine, you start with the outside fork at the place setting and work your way toward your plate. Likewise there are rules for eating sushi, and we follow them to enjoy the food and appreciate the work and passion the chef put into it. (You might even get better fish from the chef if you know the etiquette.)

The place setting in a sushi restaurant is quite simple: a plate, a bowl for dipping, and a pair of chopsticks (*hashi*). Traditional etiquette, too, is simple.

***

Chopsticks In restaurants, you'll see many people break their bamboo chopsticks apart and rub them together. This is a no-no. Just like you don't use your knife and fork to scratch each other, you don't need to do this with your chopsticks. I also see people grab their chopsticks closer to the bottom end. The proper (or elegant) way to use chopsticks is to hold them close to the top end. It looks nicer and you can pick up finer pieces of food that way.

If your chopsticks have been wrapped in paper and no chopstick rests have been provided, you can fold the wrapper to make a chopstick rest. Otherwise, use the (usually ceramic) rest provided to rest your chopsticks between courses. You can also rest your chopsticks on the small soy sauce dish.

No dismantling nigiri Never remove the fish from the rice to eat it separately. Doing so expresses disapproval of the chef's work.

Dipping in soy sauce Completely dunking your sushi in soy sauce will ruin its delicate flavor. You can do that at all-you-can-eat-type eateries to disguise artificial flavors and preservatives, but not with the sushi you make or the sushi made by skilled chefs.

No soy sauce over another sauce Speaking of soy sauce, do not dip a piece of sushi in soy sauce if it has been glazed with a sweet or citrus sauce. When a chef serves *unagi* (freshwater eel) or *anago* (saltwater eel), it is usually brushed with a sweet sauce. Adding soy sauce destroys the balance of flavors.

Adding wasabi Using too much of the green dollop of wasabi in front of you is a common mistake and disrespectful to the sushi chef. Wasabi was first used to prevent fish from going bad, somewhat like vinegar. Wasabi should not overpower the flavor of fish or the harmony of the rice and fish. Nigiri has wasabi between the rice and fish and that's enough. If you're eating sashimi, sure, you can mix wasabi into it, but, please, only a little. The proper way to do so is to use a chopstick to put a little wasabi (no bigger than a pinky nail) on the fish and dip the fish into a dish of soy sauce. High-end restaurants use real wasabi, grated from the fresh wasabi root. It's more tasty than spicy. While waiting for my food to arrive, I use my chopstick to taste the wasabi and enjoy the flavor.

Finger food It's perfectly fine to ditch the chopsticks and use your fingers instead. After all, sushi was created as finger food. Very exclusive sushi bars will provide a wet towel to clean your fingers. When I feel the chef has put their heart into making sushi for me, I use my fingers to eat it. This is my personal way of enjoying every bite of sushi and showing respect to the person who put so much time into making it for me. To eat sushi with your hands, hold the rice part of nigiri from the side and tilt it a bit to let soy sauce touch the fish but not the rice.

Taking that bite The fish—not the rice—should always touch your tongue first. Hold the nigiri and flip it so that about 20 percent of the fish touches the soy sauce. Never dip the rice, which will fall apart. Hold nigiri sushi on its sides and do not cut the piece in half. With rolls, dip one end and bite. Repeat.

Eat right away The combination of rice at the right temperature and the coldness of the fish is what makes good sushi. There is also the relationship between the vinegar on the rice and the soy sauce on the fish—all has to be well orchestrated. When it is, there is harmony. Chefs can be offended if you don't eat the sushi right away, when the harmony is just right, when the sushi is at its peak. When the customer is busy talking with fellow diners and busy drinking, the rice gets cold and the fish gets warm and the proper balance is lost. Harmony, mouthfeel, and texture are all important. Sometimes, the sushi chef will say, "Please eat," if you are too busy drinking and talking. Eat when the food is served.

Traditional sushi rolls are probably the best for entertaining. Rolls can sit out for a while and will be fine, whereas nigiri or sashimi needs to be consumed when served. At my wedding, a well-known sushi chef prepared the food. The chef did a great job and everyone loved it. The key to this great moment? The chef sourced good fish on the morning of the wedding and, once the sushi was prepared, we ate it shortly after it was on the table.

Holding nigiri correctly

Tilt the nigiri so that only about one-fourth of the fish touches the soy sauce.

Eat light to dark When we drink wine, we start with white, move to Pinot Noir, then on to more robust reds such as Cabernet Sauvignon. The proper way to eat sushi is to start with the white-fleshed, lean fish and move to the richer, oilier, darker fish. Start with fluke and seabass. Enjoy the progression of color changes as you move to the darker, richer fish. This will help educate your palate.

Ginger is a palate cleanser The pickled ginger, *gari*, on the plate should be used as a palate cleanser between types of sushi. It is not meant as a DIY garnish.

Chef knows best What's the best way to have a good relationship with your sushi chef so you learn from him and take those lessons to your home kitchen? Leave it up to the chef—*omakase* style. The chef knows what's in season and what's best that day. The chef will prepare what you like, so if you don't like sea urchin or some other type of seafood, mention it when asked, and the chef will make the course without it. *Omakase* style allows you to experience "communication," which is so often lost in our fast-paced society where almost everything can be done with your cell phone.

FUNDAMENTALS

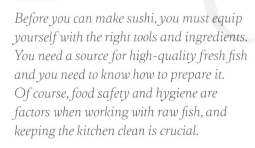

01

Before you can make sushi, you must equip
yourself with the right tools and ingredients.
You need a source for high-quality fresh fish
and you need to know how to prepare it.
Of course, food safety and hygiene are
factors when working with raw fish, and
keeping the kitchen clean is crucial.

TOOLS

———

Sushi starts with rice, so having a rice cooker is fundamental. As you will also need to cut fish and vegetables, knives and a cutting board are required. The basic tools for sushi making are found in most kitchens. You may already own many of these tools.

RICE COOKER

Rice forms the basis of sushi and, as such, I recommend making a small investment in a computerized rice cooker. You will find that, in addition to making sushi rice, you can use it to make any kind of rice. It has a function to keep rice warm at the optimal temperature, so you and your family can eat rice on the second day and it will be as fresh as "freshly steamed." All you have to do is rinse the raw rice a couple of times, add water, and hit the switch. You can choose whether your rice is firm, soft, and so on. It's automatic, so you don't have to worry about stirring or letting the steam out to keep the rice from getting mushy.

Rice cookers are relatively affordable. A decent rice cooker costs from about $50 to $80. Of course, if you want to splurge, there are high-end models that can cost upward of $200 to $300. These have different functions, such as steaming the rice as if it were cooked in a giant kettle or clay pot. I don't think you need these expensive models, but they can be nice to have. I used the same rice cooker I brought with me on my move to the United States from Japan when I was twenty-one years old, all the way until my first child was born. That was 15 years, and now my second cooker is still going strong. They last. Of course, the old-fashioned way of steaming rice in a pot works just fine, too.

CUTTING BOARDS

Wooden cutting boards look good and feel good when you're cutting fish. Wooden boards, compared to plastic cutting boards, cause less damage to your knives, too. On the other hand, even though that wood has been cut from the tree, it is still alive in a sense that it "breathes." It requires a certain level of moisture before you cut fish on it. Otherwise, food odors can penetrate the wood grain. Wash cutting boards with hot water and soap after each use.

At home, I use plastic cutting boards. These are inexpensive and you can designate them for cutting different foods, such as one for preparing fish only, one for fruit, and so one. They're also easy to clean and are dishwasher safe.

Your cutting board should be big, at least the width of your sink. Small cutting boards can be frustrating because you constantly have to move the fish around, and large fish tend to fall off small boards.

A big rice cooker

Makisu

MAKISU (BAMBOO ROLLING MAT)

Bamboo rolling mats, called *makisu* in Japanese, are not typically found in Western kitchens, but they are absolutely necessary for rolling sushi. They are inexpensive and make it easy to form perfectly round maki rolls. Bamboo sushi mats can be cleaned with a hot water and vinegar solution. This will kill any germs and protect the mat.

HASHI (CHOPSTICKS)

As already noted, you can use your fingers to eat some types of sushi because sushi was originally finger food back in the day; however, most people prefer to use chopsticks. Also, you will need chopsticks to enjoy poke bowls and other Japanese foods properly.

My wife and I carry our own hashi, which were purchased in Japan and have our names on them. We wrap them in Japanese indigo cloth (*ai-zome*) and bring them home to wash by hand. Why? Because chopsticks can be used more than once. We are not alone in this belief.

Chopsticks can be washed in a dishwasher or by hand. If you are worried about bacteria growing in the wood grains, buy chopsticks covered with lacquer paint and hand wash them.

At nicer Japanese restaurants, you will find ceramic chopstick rests so your chopsticks don't rest directly on the table or hang off the edges of plates or bowls.

Recently, I found a very cool eco-friendly product called "Cropsticks" at a sushi bar in Los Angeles. Cropsticks are made from sustainable fast-growing bamboo (most chopsticks are made of wood) with no harmful chemicals added during the production process and come with a built-in rest. The company collects used Cropsticks from restaurants and upcycles them to make home furnishings.

KNIVES

There are many types of *hocho*, "knife" in Japanese, for different purposes. The three basic types are:

Deba hocho This knife is designed to clean and fillet fish. Most likely you'll buy fish already filleted/portioned, so you may not need this knife. Deba knives have a shorter, wider blade than a Western fillet knife and they are heavier.

Santoku hocho The perfect home chef's knife, you can slice, dice, and mince meat, fish, and vegetables. It is also used for cutting maki rolls. It has the same functions as the Western chef's knife, but with a slightly different design. The santoku knife blade is typically shorter—5 to 7 inches (13 to 18 cm)—compared to the 8- to 10-inch (20 to 25 cm) Western chef's knife.

Yanagi hocho Westerners often call this knife a "sushi" knife because it is perfect for slicing fish. It has a long, narrow, very sharp blade. While other types of knives work best when you push the knife away from you, when using the yanagi hocho, you pull the blade toward you. *Be careful not to cut yourself.*

SUSHI KNIVES IN JAPAN

Highly skilled veteran chefs in Japan use knives with only one sharp side. The theory is that a knife with two sharp sides (99 percent of knives have them) breaks the fish's cell membranes, which causes the flavor of the fish to leak out. With one sharp side, the knife breaks fewer membranes. Rest assured; you don't need that level of knife for making sushi at home.

When shopping for knives, consider both the material the knife is made from and the type, or design, of the knife. A carbon-steel hocho is sharp and lasts a long time, but you have to sharpen these knives often. A stainless steel hocho, in contrast, is sharp, lasts a long time, and requires less sharpening, but is difficult to sharpen when you need to do so. I recommend a stainless steel hocho to start. If you get tired from holding knives, a ceramic hocho might be the best fit for you, as it is considerably lighter than the others. While ceramic hochos are very hard and durable against rust, these knives crack more easily than stainless steel. Plus, you can't sharpen ceramic knives with normal sharpening stones.

You'll also need a combination of knives to work with sushi. If you buy a deba hocho alone, you will not be able to make detailed cuts. If you buy a yanagi hocho alone, you will not be able to cut the bones.

BUYING SEAFOOD

The biggest challenge to making sushi is acquiring high-quality seafood. Nowhere is it truer that you get what you pay for than in the seafood industry. Sure, sometimes you find good deals when the sellers or packers must move their inventory quickly. However, overall, it takes skilled people and a certain logistical setup to maintain fresh fish at the right temperature during the entire process from catching the fish to selling it. The fish becomes "grilling grade," a considerable step down from "sushi grade," if there is one broken thread in a chilled distribution chain.

Bluefin tuna belly portions (wild) with toro

WHAT DO WE MEAN BY "SASHIMI GRADE"?

There is no standard legal definition of sashimi grade. When you see marine fish labeled as such, it simply means the seller has determined that the fish is probably good for sushi, based on an assessment of bacteria levels, temperature, parasites, appearance, smell, taste, how it's displayed, and time after being caught. For the consumer, it is a question of whether you can trust the seller.

While still alive, every fish starts out as excellent sashimi grade (unless infested by parasites known to be harmful to humans). What makes the fish sashimi grade or non-sashimi grade once it has been prepared for sale?

My answer is simple. *The distribution channel through which the fish has come determines whether the fish is suitable for raw consumption.*

So, if the fish is handled properly for raw consumption in its journey from ocean to consumer, then the fish is sashimi grade. The United States Food and Drug Administration (FDA) has guidelines for proper handling, including freezing temperatures, but states vary in their inspection and enforcement of these guidelines.

The United States' food guidelines are stricter than most other countries'. Beef, chicken, and pork are almost 100 percent ranched or farmed, and the distribution channels are uniform and controlled in terms of butchering, timing, chilling, and so forth. Plus, the meat is inspected along the way by the United States Department of Agriculture (USDA).

PARASITE RISKS

Because freshwater fish are prone to parasites, they are never labeled "sashimi grade." So any seafood you find labeled sashimi grade will be marine fish. It is most common to see tuna and farmed salmon labeled sashimi grade, but only because these are the most popular fish used in sushi. Also, tuna species—bigeye, yellowfin, bluefin, albacore, bonito, and skipjack—are generally considered safe to eat raw as long as they are kept in a sashimi-grade state appropriate for distribution. Farmed salmon is also considered parasite free when their feed is certified parasite free. All other marine species must be frozen to kill any potential parasites. The seller should do the freezing because the temperatures required to kill parasites are colder than the average temperature provided by a home freezer.

Seafood, especially fresh seafood, is still relatively new to distant markets and is not regulated—but should be. Unlike other countries, such as Spain, France, Italy, Japan, and Korea, where people have been eating raw fish for centuries, the United States is made of multiple cultures, some of which don't include raw fish in their diets. Therefore, seafood guidelines should be strict to reduce the chances of people getting sick. I suggest that the regulatory bodies in the FDA, USDA, and local health departments start defining fish for raw consumption by using the fish's distribution history as the guideline. As the consumer demand increases, we need to remove any doubt as to how the seafood was handled, so there is less risk of people getting sick from consuming seafood—raw or otherwise.

SOURCING HIGH-QUALITY SEAFOOD

When it comes to sushi, I've said this already, you get what you pay for. That's just a fact. With sushi, and with all Japanese cooking, sourcing good fish is unquestionably important. The whole point of sushi is to utilize the natural flavor of the fish. This is why freshness is so important and why we don't cover sushi with sauces that mask the scent, taste, texture, or appearance.

WHERE TO FIND HIGH-QUALITY FISH

How do you find your fish? Where do you buy it? Is wild fish better than farmed? Can good fish be found online? How do you know the fish you're buying comes from a trusted source? Is the fish at the grocery store harvested in a sustainable way? For specific recommendations, see Resources (page 163).

———

Japanese and Korean Markets Japanese and Korean markets are your best bet for finding high-quality fish. These stores sell fish mostly for raw consumption and they may have precut sushi slices on display so you don't even have to slice your purchased fish into sushi or sashimi portions. Look for "sashimi-grade" fish—although this is not a term standardized by any public health authorities. It means you can eat it raw, while "grilling grade" or "cooking grade" is what best describes fish not suitable for raw consumption.

If stores have fish cutters behind the seafood counters, ask these knowledgeable people to tell you what is in season. They'll gladly share this important information with you. Ask for a loin of tuna or salmon or sea bass or Spanish mackerel—or whatever you like to eat—to cut into sashimi blocks (called *saku*). Building relationships is key. If these fish experts know you, they'll give you a better cut of fish and a better portion. You are not expected to purchase large volumes the way chefs who patronize seafood wholesalers do. Non-Japanese and Korean Asian groceries usually don't have sashimi-grade fish available because the demand just isn't there.

———

Local Retail Seafood Markets Local seafood markets are good places to explore. Ask whether the fish you want is good for sashimi or is sashimi grade. Again, having a relationship with the people at the market can help you get nicer fish, better and extra portions, and fresher fish. Ask where the fish is from, how it was caught, and whether there are any special cooking tips. You should even be able to get ice to transport it home.

———

High-End or Organic-Focused Grocery Stores If you care whether the fish you eat has been responsibly harvested—and I hope you do after reading this book—these types of high-end markets also care very much and should tell you so right on the packaging next to the name or price tag. Because they care about distribution channels so much, the sellers at these markets are knowledgeable about many aspects of fish buying. Unfortunately, they usually don't sell fish as "sashimi grade," although sometimes you can find "sashimi grade" or "sushi grade" at these markets, too. They sell seafood as "fresh." Ask the person working at the fish counter whether the fish is good for sashimi.

———

National Chain Grocery Stores If your only choice for buying fresh fish is from seafood counters at national chains, I recommend sticking with salmon and tuna, but always ask if the fish can be eaten raw. (However, I do not recommend buying it unless the person behind the counter has the expertise to say with certainty.) Usually the national chains sell fish for cooking, and such fish is not intended for sushi use. Occasionally, you may find farmed salmon from the Faroe Islands (a self-governing region of the Kingdom of Denmark) and from Norway, Iceland, and Tasmania, which are usually good for sushi because these are countries where sashimi-grade salmon is produced and where suitable sashimi-grade distribution channels are utilized.

Grading the tuna before the auction begins

For many, many years, sushi chefs who used high-quality fish knew about the Tsukiji Fish Market in Tokyo. For decades, this market was one of the most respected names in the world for seafood sourcing. I obtained my *osakana meister*, fish master, credential in a building located in the fish market back in 2009.

When certain fish weren't available at many local fish markets in Japan, they could be found at the iconic Tsukiji. That was the power of Tsukiji. Tourists were not the priority at this market and, therefore, had to protect themselves from being hit by hundreds of mini delivery carts running swiftly throughout the stalls. The best chefs and fish buyers—the pros—visited to purchase (and negotiate hard for) what they'd use that day. All the fish from Japan that were in *shun* (peak consumption season) were available at Tsukiji. You sensed the season there. You witnessed the dedication of the fishermen who brought their fish there to challenge chefs' creativity and skills. Many fish would be kept alive during transit, sometimes arriving in a live tank with blankets wrapped around it to reduce stress from the environmental noise and light.

If you went to the market at 7 a.m., the frenzy was pretty much over, and you would not see the best of what this unique watery world had to offer. Everything was sold and nothing was carried over for the next day. Tuna was an exception. Some tuna comes in frozen even before rigor mortis sets in. People can recall every January 5, the first auction after the market closed for the holidays, when some tuna sold for more than the price of a nice house.

Tsukiji wasn't merely a fish market. Dry goods, high-end knives, seaweed—everything you needed—was sold there. It was a place where passion and desire were intertwined to create fish as the triumph of the food chain. Fish was king there, not humans . . .

Why I am using past tense here? Sadly, Tsukiji closed in October 2018. The market moved to a different location called Toyosu. The new building is temperature controlled and has a designated area for tourists. It's wonderful that you don't have to worry about being hit by a tricycle loaded with fish anymore, though I sure do miss hearing the shouting fishmongers, telling you, "Get the hell out my way!"

BUYING FRESH OR FROZEN?

Of course, fresh-off-the-boat seafood is better than frozen because fresh fish still has all its flavor intact. That said, much of the so-called "fresh seafood" you may buy or are served at even a high-end sushi restaurant may have been frozen at one time.

All fish have their seasons when they can and cannot be legally caught. This is to protect the fisheries while the fish are spawning. In the Atlantic Ocean, for example, the season for bluefin tuna is spring to early fall, depending on when they reach the quota that year. So, if you want to enjoy Atlantic bluefin in the winter, chances are it has been frozen.

The problem with frozen fish is that when the cell membranes break down, the flavor is lost. We can literally see the outcome. We call this the "drip"—the moisture that comes off the fish contains all the fish's umami flavor. However, since the 1980s, when flash freezing was developed to preserve the catch on long trips, freezing is no longer the problem it once was.

Variously called blast freezing, super freezing, or flash freezing, this process keeps the fish's taste intact if it is frozen right out of the water. The temperature of the fish is rapidly lowered to −76°F to −112°F (−60°C to −80°C) so the cell membranes are not broken. If you see fish identified as flash frozen, use it for sushi. There are various ways to defrost such fish, but the best way is to thaw it in your refrigerator overnight.

Flash freezing keeps seafood fresh, fresher than what you might find "fresh" at the market because *that* fresh seafood has already been at the market a couple of days. Because this is all such a high-tech process requiring an even lower frozen-temperature distribution channel than usual, the cost of flash-frozen fish is greater than regular frozen fish, but less than fresh fish that has been flown in by air.

Many seafood products distributed in Japan are processed by flash freezing. Japan has the infrastructure throughout the country to provide cold storage and the necessary temperature of −58°F to −76°F (−50°C to −60°C). Most restaurants in Japan have these super freezers. In other parts of the world, including the United States, restaurants don't have these freezers in use as often.

The rigor mortis phase begins when you bring flash-frozen fish home. It is, therefore, very important that the fish be defrosted slowly in the refrigerator to avoid excessive drip loss.

Fresh fish is the best, as long as the fish has come from a sashimi distribution channel. Make sure to keep the fish chilled to less than 40°F (4.4°C) during the time you travel home from the retailer. Ask for a bag of ice or bring ice and a cooler with you.

ADVICE FOR BUYING SEAFOOD FOR SASHIMI

Whatever fish you buy, you should be able to use your senses to determine whether the fish is as fresh as advertised. Here's what to look for:

––––––

Smell The fish should not have any unpleasant or "fishy" smell. It should smell clean.

––––––

Touch If the flesh is pressed, it should be firm and springy, not spongy or sticky.

––––––

Whole fish appearance If you are buying a whole fish, the eyes should be clear and plump, not cloudy or sunken. The gills should be red, never dark or murky looking.

Tuna

Tuna is one of the most popular fish among both Japanese and non-Japanese people. At sushi bars, some chefs are not happy on the days when the tuna is not good—even if all of the other fish they are serving up that day are good quality. Of course, the opposite is also true. My point here is: Sourcing good tuna is imperative for success in your sushi adventure. But not all tuna are created the same.

TYPES OF TUNA

The tuna family is quite large and includes many species, but there are only a few you are likely to use to make sushi: bluefin, bigeye, yellowfin, and albacore.

_____

Bluefin Tuna Bluefin tuna are a cold-water fish, some of which migrate several oceans to find a comfortable water temperature. They are the largest tuna and can weigh up to 1,000 pounds (454 kg). The flesh ranges from pretty dark (the leanest part of the loin) to lightly colored (the *toro*, or oiliest part of the belly). Bluefin's toro is widely regarded as the tastiest; it is also relatively expensive. A fresh piece of bluefin *o-toro* (the super-fatty tuna belly) should almost melt in the mouth. Southern bluefin tuna is a similar species, but it only grows up to 300 pounds (136 kg) and is harvested in the Southern Hemisphere. They are usually then ranched and shipped to the United States, Asia, and Europe.

_____

Bigeye Tuna Bigeye tuna can come from various oceans, but they do not migrate as far a distance as bluefin tuna do. Its texture and flavor depend on its size and where it was caught, in addition to the season. Just like bluefin tuna, bigeye tuna o-toro comes from the belly. Compared to yellowfin tuna, most of the bigeye tuna is meatier and darker in color.

_____

Yellowfin Tuna The flavor of yellowfin tuna is lighter and more refreshing than that of bigeye tuna. In Japan, people tend to consume this tuna during the hot summer months. Yellowfin is less expensive than bluefin and bigeye, as it is harvested in almost all warm-water regions.

_____

Albacore Tuna Albacore tuna is a smaller tuna, with light-colored flesh. It is caught in both warm and cold waters. The albacore tuna harvested in warm water is usually called "pink albacore." It's lean and refreshing to eat during warmer months. Albacore tuna harvested in cold water is usually quite fatty, and called *toro bincho* ("toro" describes the velvety, soft, oily part of a fish; *bincho* means albacore tuna in Japanese—hence, albacore tuna's fatty belly section). Oily albacore tuna used to go only to Japan years ago, but some of them come to the United States today through frozen distribution channels.

Both pink albacore tuna (chilled) and toro albacore tuna flesh are very soft, especially toro (always sold frozen and skin-off in vacuum packs). You have to slice them when not completely thawed or you end up with chunks. You can purchase pink albacore tuna year-round at mainstream seafood markets. Toro bincho can be found at Japanese and Korean markets; they come frozen as 2- to 3-pound (908 g to 1.3 kg) loins.

You can use your fingers to measure the "toro" level of a fish.

ASSESSING TUNA

Fresh tuna should be judged by its size, color, odor, texture, and certification. Tuna portions, called *toro*, may be classified as *o-toro* (super-fatty tuna belly) and *chutoro* (medium fatty tuna belly). *Akami*, found in the non-fatty portion of the belly side or on the back loins of the fish, is lean red meat with a taste and texture almost like very rare filet mignon.

Size A big fish's sinews are about ¹/₂ to 1 inch (1 to 2.5 cm) apart; smaller fish have less space between the sinews. If the store displays loins of fish, imagine putting four of them together to create a "log" to see, for instance, the full size of a tuna. When fillets are displayed, observe how wide the fillets are (the shorter edge).

When a fish is too small there is less flavor, but the fish may be good for salads with dressing. When a fish is big, there is more acidity in the flesh and an iron taste is present, which works well with some red wines and sauces. For sushi, 15- to 25-pound (6.8 to 11.3 kg) loins are optimal—but I don't want to promote this idea and I dislike it when chefs pick fish based only on size because it is not a sustainable practice. With the size of the bait and depth of its placement, fishermen can control the size of the fish they catch to a certain extent (a fishing method called longline; see page 34). But beyond that, it is up to the consumer to appreciate tuna in whatever size nature offers.

Color Some tuna, especially bigeye tuna or bluefin tuna from Asia, can appear burgundy red, a red bean color. Yellowfin tuna is a lighter red, almost a pink Champagne red, but it is not fluorescent pink or bright red. If the fish is that garishly colored, then the original tuna was junk to begin with and has gone through a coloring process that involves carbon monoxide. You'll be eating something mushy with no flavor. I wouldn't recommend that fish.

Smell *Fresh fish should not smell.* The color of the flesh can be darker in fish for raw consumption, but the flesh shouldn't have a strong odor. Odor is caused by bacteria; if the fish had bacterial growth, it is likely the fish went through a phase or two of temperature abuse. A slight smell is okay, but it should not be something that makes you uncomfortable. Such fish are for cooking or frying—not for sushi!

Texture If you can touch the flesh before you purchase it—which is not often the case—a feeling of resiliency is key. The flesh should have the softness of a fresh mozzarella ball, not a rotten tomato.

Price Too good to be true is too good to be true. When the tuna is inexpensive and the color is bright pink, I'm sorry . . . it's not a good piece of fish and was probably treated with carbon monoxide. The most expensive part of the fish, the belly portion, or toro, is such because it's also the most sought-after part of the fish for sushi.

Certification Marine Stewardship Council (MSC) certification is a good guideline to follow. The MSC supports fisheries trying to do the right thing, meaning the fish they certify are wild, traceable, and sustainable. Their distinctive blue fish label is only applied to wild fish or seafood from fisheries certified to the MSC Fisheries Standard, a science-based set of requirements for sustainable fishing. You can find the label on packaged frozen fish or on tags at the seafood counter. Ask about it if you don't see it. According to the MSC website, around the world, you'll find the blue fish label on more than thirty thousand products and menus in almost one hundred countries.

TUNA FISHING METHODS

Not all tuna is the same in terms of their fishery's sustainability. Knowing how the tuna was caught will help you make an intelligent choice.

Handline/Pole and Line

How does the saying go? A fisherman uses his line to catch one fish at a time. So it is in the Maldives and the Philippines, where tuna is caught with a pole and a line. Tuna tends to fight on the hook, so the meat quality is not always optimal. This is sustainable fishing, but it's not a realistic method for supplying all the tuna in demand in today's world. In fact, less than 10 percent of the global tuna catch comes from this method.

Longline

Most tuna used for sushi is caught using the longline method. With this method, several miles of line is laid with hooks 2 to 3 feet (0.6 to 0.9 m) apart. Depending on the size of the baitfish, the depth at which the bait is dropped, and any equipment used to prevent sea turtles or seabirds from getting hooked, fishermen can target specific sizes of tuna and reduce accidental bycatches. This is a responsible fishing method. Fish are individually graded and iced to maintain the highest quality possible. About 18 percent of the global tuna catch results from the longline method.

Purse Seiner

The most popular method of catching tuna by far is this high-tech catching method. Three-quarters of the global tuna catch, including tuna found in cans, comes from these massive fishing campaigns that utilize giant ships and spotter planes. To envision this method, imagine a purse with strings: You lay out a vertical fish net curtain that is miles long in order to cover a school of tuna. Then, you squeeze the curtain and catch everything and anything in the net's path. Whatever is in the net—immature tuna, sea turtles, dolphins, whatever—is then sold according to weight. The purse seiner industry has improved its practice in recent years, but scientists at the United Nations' Food and Agriculture Organization concluded in one report that no matter how we tighten the regulation against longliners, it wouldn't improve global tuna fishery conditions, because the fish that wasn't caught by the longliner fleet will be caught by the purse seiner boats.

FARMED OR WILD?

Most bluefin tuna sold today is wild; however, because it is so desirable, the amount of tuna in the wild is being depleted. Though efforts are being made to create a sustainable farming system, I must warn you: Some bluefin tuna are "ranched," which is often mistaken as "farmed." There is only one brand of "farmed" bluefin tuna available in the world today—KINDAI Tuna from Japan.

Most of the so-called "farmed" bluefin tuna are not actually farmed; they are technically "ranched," and ranching does harm the wild population. Fishermen catch wild bluefin and tow them in nets, alive, and then release them into the farming pens. While in the farming pens, the fish are fed the fattiest feeds (sardines) to allow them to gain fat as quickly as possible, which put lots of stress on the fish. While most bluefin tuna ranchers do adhere to strict guidelines as to how much they can catch each season for this purpose, illegal catches have still been reported and they are not as small in volume as we all hope.

The truly farmed brand of bluefin tuna, KINDAI Tuna from Japan, is raised from eggs taken from mature Kindai tuna and transferred to pens, where they reach market size. These fish are expensive, but the farms have been working toward lowering the cost by feeding them pellets to reduce reliance on other fish. Researchers at Kindai University in Japan have been implementing insect- and plant-based proteins in the feed as well.

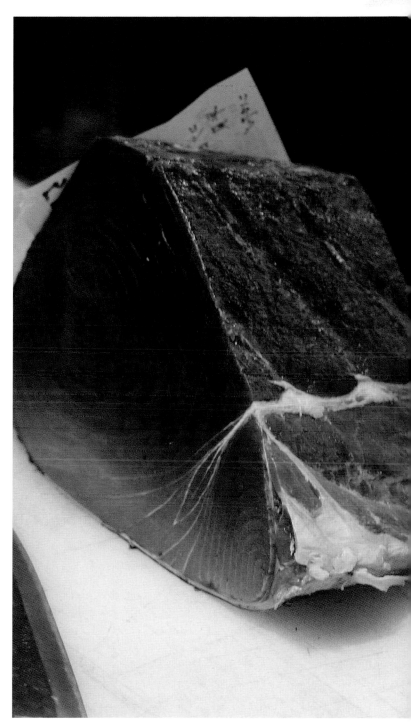

Salmon (Sake)

Salmon is known as *sake* in Japanese (not to be confused with sake, the alcoholic beverage appropriate to drink with sushi). Salmon is one of the most consumed seafoods in the United States.

TYPES OF SALMON

Most of the salmon used for sushi is farmed Atlantic salmon. While wild salmon is tasty, it may not be the optimal choice for sushi. I will explain why later in this section.

Atlantic Salmon Virtually all Atlantic salmon is farmed, though not necessarily in the Atlantic Ocean. Atlantic salmon is the species name. Such salmon may be called farmed salmon, Chilean salmon, Norwegian salmon, or Scottish salmon. In the case of "Scottish salmon," for example, the correct name should be "Atlantic salmon farmed in Scottish waters." Farmed Atlantic salmon is suitable to eat raw when distributed as "sashimi grade" because there is a lot of transparency in how the fish was raised.

Pacific Salmon Several species of salmon can be found in the Pacific Ocean. I do not encourage using Pacific salmon for making sushi at home. It is difficult to find a trusted supplier who understands and maintains a sashimi-grade supply chain. Experienced sushi chefs who do serve Pacific salmon usually take extra care in preparing it. The five main types of Pacific salmon are:

Chinook Also called king salmon, this is the largest and fattiest of the Pacific salmon.

Sockeye The flesh has a deep reddish color and is lower in fat than some species, but high in flavor.

Coho Also called silver salmon, this is the most widely available wild fresh salmon caught in the fall.

Pink Also called humpback salmon, this fish is a pale, pinkish-gray color with a delicate flavor, and is mostly used for the canning industry.

Chum With pink flesh not particularly high in fat, this may also be called dog salmon because it was traditionally fed to sled dogs. Its roe is the most valued of the five varieties because of its size and flavor. After being strained and separated, the eggs are used to make ikura—the familiar fat, bright-orange pearls in sushi rolls.

ASSESSING SALMON

The information about salmon at retail stores can be confusing and can lead to buying the wrong fish. Use these guidelines when selecting your salmon for purchase.

Size The larger the fish, the oilier the flesh. Of course, farmed salmon are soft and oily throughout regardless of size. Still, if you prefer oilier fish, seek bigger fish. If you like leaner fish (like wild salmon), go for a smaller size. Regardless of size, though, because ocean-farmed salmon have been couch potatoes from birth, even small fish have a high fat content.

Color Reddish-orange is more visually appealing to our eyes than yellowish-orange flesh. Salmon farmers are able to manipulate the color of the flesh by adapting what the fish eat. In general, fish are fed naturally occurring or synthetically produced carotenoids to add more red color. There is nothing harmful here (the carotenoids may even have anti-inflammatory properties), but our wallets suffer because this adds cost to make the salmon look good. For this reason, yellowish-orange salmon are usually less expensive than those that are deep pink or red.

Smell Again, *fresh fish does not smell.* If you could have gone to the world-famous Tsukiji Fish Market in Tokyo, you would never feel as though you were inside the belly of a smelly fish. Even at sushi fish wholesalers in the United States, there is no smell. Sashimi-grade fish should not smell fishy. If you go to seafood wholesalers who handle fish for grilling, most fish do not smell either. Fresh fish doesn't smell, although fish intended for frying does, sometimes.

Because most salmon we can buy are farm raised, they have a higher oil content than wild-caught salmon. Higher fat content means the fish will start to smell faster. However, most retailers and their distributors know how to keep the fish at the proper temperature, so farmed salmon shouldn't stink. In other words, if salmon smells badly from 2 feet (60 cm) away, don't buy it. That might be the old stuff, and the new fish may be in the back.

Texture Farmed Atlantic salmon is soft in the first place, so it's hard to tell whether it's good just by pushing on it (unless there is no bounce back at all). Consider all the other factors noted for assessing the fish.

Price Salmon from Scotland and salmon from the Faroe Islands are the most expensive. Icelandic salmon is getting up there in price, too. Norwegian salmon is less costly than Scottish, and some are good in both flavor and with regard to sustainability. Chilean salmon suffered major disease outbreaks within the last decade and the government stepped in to control the safety and quality of their farmed salmon. Canadian salmon once had a bad rap, but they cleaned up their operation and it is much better now than before.

Certification Aquaculture Stewardship Council (ASC) certification is a good way to tell whether something is fresh. However, farmed Atlantic salmon is not in danger of extinction. So pay attention to the way the fish was raised, such as what drugs were used and the meat-to-feed conversion ratio (see page 40). Overcrowding in farming cages causes stress, which leads to disease. To suppress the potential disease outbreaks, farmers sometimes use antibiotics at lower-end salmon farms. But, the use of growth hormones has almost disappeared at salmon-farming operations, even for lower-end products.

While it's not always possible, or obvious, how a fish was raised, when you see a farm-raised Atlantic salmon with a brand name, you can go to their website to learn what was or was not administrated to the fish, the meat-to-feed conversion ratio, what's in the feed, etc.

When the fish has no brand name (in most cases), farm-raised Atlantic salmon harvested in Scottish (including the Faroe Islands), Norwegian, Icelandic (for farmed king salmon), New Zealand, and Tasmania waters are safe bets. These countries have specific standards and we can feel good about eating fish that was raised in a socially responsible manner.

I recommend asking the person selling the fish these questions. If they don't know the answer, then that business establishment most likely doesn't sell fish with "good grades," simply because they don't care about how it was raised and where. Yet, here is my argument: Which is better for your health? Eating beef or chicken or eating salmon raised with antibiotics?

FARMED OR WILD?

Your choice at the seafood counter is often farmed or wild-caught salmon. Wild-caught salmon tastes great in the peak season, June through September. At that point, its muscle is toned and its fat content is at its lifetime high because the salmon is ready to take a long journey to return to its spawning grounds. Beware of any salmon labeled wild-caught outside of its season. Wild-caught salmon must be frozen to eliminate any parasites (see page 24).

Ocean Farmed Most fresh salmon sold at stores are ocean-farmed Atlantic salmon. Your choice will likely be fillets, with or without the skin, or steaks. Unlike tuna skin, salmon skin can be tasty when crisped in a frying pan and enjoyed in a roll or rice bowl.

Inland-Farmed Salmon Inland-farmed salmon are now available. These operations affect the environment less than the open-water oceanic salmon farms, so availability of fish from these origins is slowly growing. Of course, the fish can't grow as big as those ocean-farmed due to the confined space in which they are kept. However, the technology is improving rapidly and the fish quality is also improving. If you feel farmed Atlantic salmon is too greasy, these fish might be your choice as they stay lean.

MEAT-TO-FEED RATIO CONVERSION

The meat-to-feed conversion ratio is the relationship between how much feed is required for the fish to gain 1 pound (454 g) of body weight. So, for example, high-end farmed Atlantic salmon achieve close to a 1:1 ratio (1 pound, or 454 g, of feed for the fish to gain 1 pound, or 454 g, of body weight). While these might be relatively expensive, I would say 1:1½ is a good ratio (1½ pounds, or 681 g, of feed for a gain of 1 pound, or 454 g, of body weight).

Regarding feed, this has been the area where the Atlantic salmon industry has improved drastically within the last few years. Lots of modern technologies have been introduced to obtain not only healthier sustainable protein feed but also feed less harmful to the environment.

Buri and Hamachi
(Japanese Yellowtail)

Because the common names of fish are often used indiscriminately, it can be difficult to figure out what is actually on a menu, particularly in less expensive sushi restaurants. Even fish pros make this mistake. Nowhere is this more true than among the yellowtail family. *Buri* (wild) and *hamachi* (farmed) are actually the same fish—a Japanese yellowtail. Hamachi is aquacultured and typically has a soft texture with full flavor. Buri is typically exported from Japan in *shun*, or peak season, which is late November to mid-March. It has firmer flesh than hamachi and a refreshing richness that lingers in your mouth. By its DNA design, hamachi/buri has the highest oil content when compared to its two siblings, *kanpachi* and *hiramasa*.

Note that there are hamachi that have had carbon monoxide used to keep the flesh white and bloodline red in color. It is imperative to go to a trusted source, which I list in this book (see page 163).

Kanpachi, sometimes called amberjack, is found in warm waters and can grow very large, weighing as much as 200 pounds (91 kg). Kanpachi is farmed in Japan, Hawaii, and the European Union and some are now being aquacultured inland in the mainland United States. This fish has a cleaner taste and slightly firmer texture than farmed hamachi.

Hiramasa is the yellowtail local to the West Coast of the United States. It's low cost with not much flavor, so it works well with a variety of sauces (see Yellowtail with Beet Green Relish, page 96). It has a firm flesh and a more linear shape than kanpachi or hamachi/buri. Farmed yellowtail from Australia, called "king fish," is hiramasa. They are smaller in size than hamachi/buri or kanpachi (3 to 4 pounds, or 1.3 to 1.8 kg).

Hirame (Fluke or Halibut)

Many fish used for sushi belong to the category called hirame, including halibut. The Japanese word *hirame* means "flat eye," and, in Japan, the hirame typically served is Japanese flounder. In North American sushi restaurants, hirame may be flounder, fluke, or halibut. Adding to the confusion, fluke is also called summer flounder because it is most abundant in summer. All flukes are flounders, but not all flounders are flukes. The way to tell whether you have a winter flounder (called flounder) or summer flounder (called fluke) is to see which side of the fish has both eyes. The winter flounder has its eyes on the right side and has a small mouth; summer flounder (fluke) has its eyes on the left side and has a large toothy mouth.

Fluke and flounder can be purchased whole, while Alaskan halibut can be large and are more likely to be sold as steaks. Atlantic halibut is endangered, so buy farmed halibut or wild-caught Pacific halibut when in season, historically from March to September. Farmed fluke imported from Japan are great quality but expensive; Korean farmed fluke is more affordable but can be very oily. There are many local varieties that can be found at reasonable price points.

If your local seafood outlet displays whole fish, you can ask them to fillet one for you. Unlike tuna and salmon, these fillets for grilling will be the same for sashimi use.

Unagi

Have you tasted a muddy undertone in the unagi you bought? Was its skin so thick and chewy you thought you were biting rubber? Let's avoid that from now on when purchasing unagi.

Most often, you will find frozen *unagi kabayaki* (meaning "grilled eel fillets") ranging from 6 to 14 ounces (170 to 400 g). The most suitable size for nigiri sushi is 8 to 9 ounces (225 to 255 g). The skin starts to get stiffer on bigger fillets, but smaller fillets may not be flavorful enough. Unagi from Japan is very expensive.

When Chef Nozawa (co-owner and co-founder of the Sugarfish Empire) was teaching me how to pick good unagi more than twenty years ago, he said, "Hold the frozen unagi kabayaki piece in the middle; you want a piece that is thick in the middle." I started practicing that when I picked unagi for his restaurant. I don't think there is anyone who can say they have had bad unagi at the famed Sushi Nozawa restaurant back in the day. Picking pieces that are thick in the middle ensures you get flavorful unagi at home.

Uni (Sea Urchin)

Sea urchin isn't a popular seafood in America, so buying uni can be challenging. The edible parts of the spiny sea urchin are the lobes of orange-yellow roe (technically gonads, not roe) within the shell. Many who say, "I don't like uni," have had bad experiences with it. Even I have experienced bad uni—and not just once. This brutal economic principle is in place for uni: cheap ones are bad (make me want to throw up) and expensive ones are good (unless they are not in season). Uni should be creamy in texture, tasting slightly sweet and slightly briny.

In coastal California, sea urchins grow from May through August, so a very limited harvesting volume is allowed then; peak season is September through March. You can find uni out of season because processors try to keep them alive in their fish tanks, but they lose their rich flavor as a result. In recent years, uni production has been reduced in California's coastal waters because there is not enough good kelp for sea urchins to eat, according to Dave Rudie, owner of Catalina Offshore Products in San Diego, who has been promoting the recovery of the local ocean region for decades.

Making uni sushi is heavily dependent on the uni's quality because it is served raw without any sauce other than soy sauce and wasabi.

When buying uni, look for those from San Diego and Santa Barbara. Japanese uni is good, but expensive, and sometimes has a very strong reef flavor, which some people find unpleasant. Uni from Maine and Chile used to taste of chemicals, but they have been producing pretty good products lately. You can buy live sea urchins or already prepared uni. If buying prepared uni (just the edible lobes), look for uni with white sticky stuff at the top of some pieces (though you might not find this often). Based on my experience (with no scientific explanation), those are tasty. Also, look for those that are orange-yellow, rather than brownish-yellow. Freshness is indicated by clearly defined grains; those with runny grains may taste fine, but their shelf life will be shorter and they should be eaten immediately.

If you are a fan of uni, visit high-end sushi bars and tell the chef you want to try uni from different regions side by side. It'll take your uni infatuation to the next level.

称	生うに(生食用)	加工者	羽立水産
産地	北海道産		北海道茅部
材料	うに・食塩・ミョウバン		字砂原 2-
存方法	10℃以下にて保存	ホームページ	http://www.ha

Store-bought uni

INGREDIENTS

———

The basic ingredients used to make sushi are seafood and rice flavored with vinegar, sugar, and salt. Western sushi is sometimes wrapped in seaweed, tofu skin, or very thinly sliced cucumber. It may be flavored or served with a host of condiments, and these go beyond the usual soy sauce and wasabi.

RICE

For making sushi, we use short-grain white rice because it is stickier than long-grain rice and will hold the sushi together better. The proper rice to buy for making sushi is polished short-grain Japanese rice or medium-grain California rice. These types of rice are often labeled as sushi rice, or Calrose rice at stores in the United States.

NORI

Nori is edible red algae, usually sold in dried, roasted sheets. It is made like paper, with shredded bits pressed into a frame and then dried. High-quality nori is smooth and uniform in texture, with a dark-green color, and should have a slight scent of the ocean. The flavor is lightly smoky and briny. Experienced sushi chefs will sear a nori sheet right before using it for sushi. This adds a savory umami aroma that is enhanced by the vinegar in the sushi rice.

Avoid nori that is splotchy, crumbly, pale green, or reddish. If you don't make sushi with nori regularly, keep the nori fresh by storing it in an airtight container in the freezer for up to 6 months. When you are ready to use the nori, pass it quickly over an open flame to restore its crisp texture.

Roasted seaweed is called sushi nori, or *yaki nori* in Japanese. Shredded nori, known as *kizami nori*, is used as a garnish for rice bowls and poke.

CONDIMENTS AND FLAVORINGS

In the Japanese pantry, certain ingredients add kick, zing, and umami to our dishes. Many are easily found in most large supermarkets. Here are the ingredients you need to make the recipes in this book.

———

Daikon Oroshi (Grated Daikon Radish) Grated daikon radish cuts greasiness from food and lends a touch of sweetness, especially when used with dashi-based soups and sauces. Daikon radish doesn't need to be peeled, but you can if you prefer. Much of daikon's sharp flavor is in the peel. If you are making sushi and want to grate the daikon in advance, prevent it from browning by keeping it submerged in a bowl of acidulated water (1 cup, or 240 ml, water plus 1 tablespoon, or 15 ml, rice vinegar or lemon juice). When ready to use the daikon, remove it from the water, squeeze out any excess liquid, and plate.

Goma (Roasted Sesame Seeds) Japanese restaurants use a lot of this ingredient, both the black and the white seeds. They can be incorporated into a sauce or ground and combined with tofu and other ingredients. Roasted seeds are often sprinkled over sushi rolls to add a crunchy texture.

Goma Abura (Sesame Oil) Pressed from toasted sesame seeds, sesame oil is essential for frying, sautéing, and stir-frying. It is also sometimes used for marinating. There is a zero-cholesterol version with virtually no difference in flavor available from a Japanese manufacturer and the Japanese grocery chains listed in Resources (page 163).

Miso Miso is made by fermenting soybeans. Red miso is typically made from soybeans fermented with barley or other grains, with a higher percentage of soybeans and/or a longer fermentation period. It can range in color from red to dark brown and its flavor is more assertive than that of white miso. With white miso, the soybeans are augmented with a large percentage of rice koji (yeast), which results in a color that ranges from white to light beige. The flavor has a definite sweetness from the rice koji. White miso contains less sodium than red miso. Usually in the Tokyo area you find red miso, whereas people in the Osaka area prefer white miso.

Ponzu Sauce An all-purpose base for many Japanese sauces, ponzu sauce (see page 159 for recipe) is made from rice vinegar, dashi, mirin, and yuzu (a Japanese citrus fruit). Light and healthy, the sauce pairs well with meat, seafood, and veggies.

Sansho Made from the tiny unripened berries of the Japanese prickly ash, these little green pods are packed with a subtle sweet citrus flavor and a tongue-numbing tingle. It is commonly sprinkled on noodles, soups, and *unagi kabayaki* (grilled farmed freshwater eel) and *yakitori* (grilled chicken on skewers).

Shichimi Togarashi (Japanese Seven-Spice Blend) This popular Japanese seasoning is a mixture of seven different ingredients ground together and sold in a small bottle. A typical blend may contain any combination of coarsely ground red chile pepper (the main ingredient), ground sansho, roasted orange peel, black and white sesame seeds, hemp seeds, dried ginger, nori, and poppy seeds. I sprinkle this over soups (especially hot soups), noodles, yakitori, grilled fish or chicken . . . or onto anything to add a bit of zest.

Shiso (Perilla Leaf) I love this leaf—a member of the mint family that offers hints of citrus. This is Japanese "basil" and goes well with fish, poultry, and tempura. Shiso plants also go by the name beefsteak plant. You can often find bunches of green shiso leaves packaged in foam trays in Japan's food markets. It's easy to grow in your backyard (though it is as invasive as mint) or on a sunny balcony. My mother used to ask me to harvest shiso from the backyard and make tempura with it. Simple, healthy, and delicious!

Shoga (Ginger) Fresh ginger root (*shoga*; actually a rhizome) is commonly prepared thinly sliced and pickled, at which time it is known as *gari*. Pickled ginger is served alongside sushi and should be eaten as a palate cleanser between bites.

Shoyu (Soy Sauce) Soy sauce is *shoyu* in Japanese. While there are close to one hundred different types, they all are made from soybeans. Most use wheat in their production, but there are some gluten-free and low-sodium versions available; generally, tamari is gluten-free. *Usukuchi* soy sauce is lighter in color than other soy sauces, but not lighter in flavor, and may have a higher sodium content.

Su (Vinegar) Rice vinegar, sometimes called rice wine vinegar, is typically used as a seasoning for sushi rice, along with sugar and salt. In most American markets, the choices are plain rice vinegar and seasoned rice vinegar, which may contain sugar, sometimes corn syrup, and salt or MSG. You may also encounter sushi vinegar, which is ready to use in sushi. The recipes in this book all call for plain rice vinegar.

Fresh wasabi roots

Making wasabi paste by mixing the powder form with water

Wasabi (Japanese Horseradish) Wasabi can be purchased as a powder, paste, chopped pieces, or fresh root. The higher the cost, the less hot or spicy it is. Freshly grated wasabi root is not really hot, but rather very flavorful, and I like to eat it on its own. Wasabi became a part of sushi because of its ability to control bacterial growth back when refrigeration was not available in Japan. For the recipes here, buy powdered wasabi and mix it into a paste with water—you won't need much.

Yuzu Yuzu is a unique citrus fruit with a flavor reminiscent of lemon but less sharp and fruitier. The golf ball–size yuzu provides both juice and zest to enhance sauces, including ponzu sauce and vinegars. Yuzu is widely available in the States thanks to the Nagatoshi family in Oxnard, California, who spent years cultivating it. When buying fresh yuzu, select fairly firm, fragrant fruit. Store yuzu at room temperature for 1 to 2 weeks, or refrigerate it for longer storage.

Yuzu Kosho (Yuzu Pepper Paste) Made from fermented fresh chiles and yuzu juice, yuzu pepper paste is citrusy and a bit spicy. Use a pinky nail–size morsel of this on white-fleshed fish and grilled chicken, or to add extra flavor to any dish.

FISH PREPARATION

Preparation is extremely important in sushi making. A number of saku (see page 58) portions of fish resting inside the glass showcase at sushi bars look simple, but the chefs worked for hours to prepare them. I will show you how to prepare fish for sushi.

When working with raw fish, a clean environment is the number one priority to avoid exposure to bacteria or potential cross-contamination. Begin your fish preparation by scrubbing your kitchen to make a clean environment. You will also need:

Knife (see page 20)

Cutting board (see page 18)

Clean kitchen towels

For the best results, use a hocho (knife) and smoothly pull toward you with each slice. The worst thing you can do is to apply the tip of the hocho at the far corner of the saku (away from your body) and grind the knife as if you are using a saw. The fish flesh will be separated from each sinew and lose its shape.

After each cut with the knife, wipe your knife clean. Keep your cutting surface clean by wiping it frequently with a damp cloth. Collect fish trimmings in one container and your sushi and sashimi pieces in another.

Chutoro, medium-marbled belly of ranched bluefin tuna from Spain

Gorgeous wild bluefin tuna belly loin

HYGIENE AND FOOD SAFETY

Good hygiene and food safety go hand in hand. Although the United States is considered fairly obsessed with hygiene, they are rated number two in the world behind Japan. Without the healthy, clean environment in Japan, there could have been many sick people over the years as so much raw fish is prepared and eaten there.

Most seafood wholesalers in the United States do a great job keeping things clean. After the daily fish processing is over, chlorinated hot water is used to wash the walls, tables, and floors. Workers wear hairnets while fish cutters wear silicone gloves and rubber boots designated to be worn on the processing floors. When you visit a processing company, you are asked to wear the "doctor's coat," a hairnet, a mask to cover your mouth, and rubber boots and then asked to step into chlorinated water. Finally, you walk into a small room where jet air comes out of hundreds of holes to dust off your clothes, much like the tornado machine your kids can experience at arcades. At some of the most rigorous processing plants I've been to, in Japan and the Maldives, I wouldn't have doubted it if someone told me they were manufacturing fine Swiss watches or computer CPUs. They were that clean. No dust. No conversation. There was virtually no chance for harmful bacteria to fall on the fish they were processing.

The fish you buy to eat at home has gone through an integrated distribution channel with rigorous safety standards, especially if you purchase from the sources listed in this book. I'm not asking you to wear a space suit or telling you not to breathe while preparing your fish. I'm just asking you to be aware and use common sense. Pay attention to the following three key factors at all times:

———

Temperature Do not let raw fish sit at room temperature for more than 20 minutes.

———

Smell Sashimi-grade fish should smell clean and fresh with no "fishy" odor.

———

Avoid cross-contamination Do not use the same knife or cutting board for fish that has touched poultry or some other meat that can cause cross-contamination.

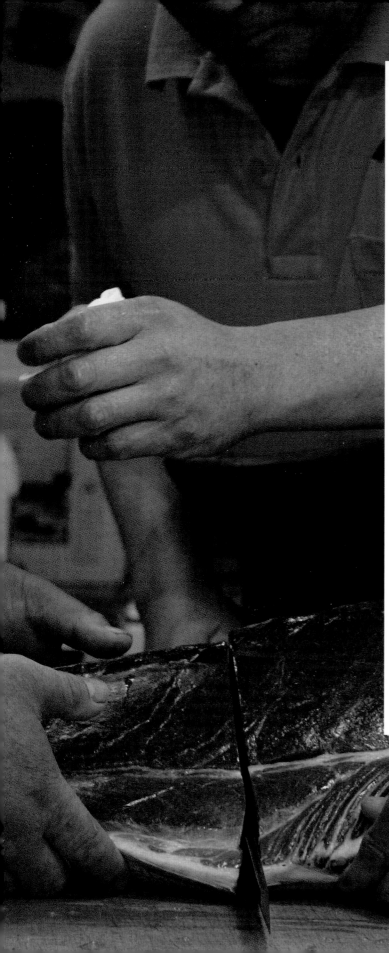

TUNA

Most likely you will purchase rectangular strips of tuna (7 to 8 inches, or 18 to 20 cm, long and 1¹/₂ to 2 inches, or 3.5 to 5 cm, wide), called *saku*, or you will purchase a portion of whole loin, often called a block, from which you can cut your own saku. The sharper the knife, the less damage is done to the flesh's cells, which helps keep the flavor intact.

Cutting Tuna Loin into Saku Strips

01   Ask your fishmonger for a saku strip portion or "block" of a whole loin.

02   Trim off the uneven portion of the tip of the block.

03   Trim off the uneven portion on the side of the block.

04   Slice off the top of the block at the point where the sinews are close together.

05   Now you have two pieces, one roughly rectangular in shape with the skin attached, and one smaller and triangular in shape.

06   Remove the skin from the bottom rectangular piece and cut from it saku strips approximately 1 inch (2.5 cm) wide.

07   When your knife hits the cutting board, tilt it a bit and separate the saku strip from the remaining portion. Repeat this movement until you have divided the whole bottom portion into saku strips.

08   Continue cutting saku strips from the top triangular portion. This section will have some thicker tendons. Adjust the shape of your saku to follow the tendon, and remove it.

09   Each of your saku should be of similar size.

01

02

03

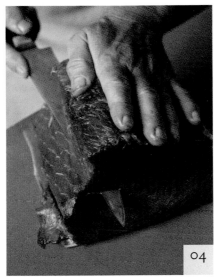

04

05

06

07

08

09

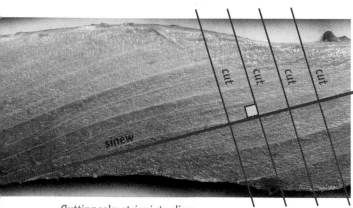

01

Cutting saku strips into slices

Cutting Saku Strips into Slices

Place the thicker end of a saku strip away from you, checking that the sinews run diagonally from the top right corner to bottom left corner. Make $\frac{1}{2}$-inch (1 cm) slices at a 90-degree angle to the sinews. Pull the knife toward you, not away from you, so the sashimi won't be chewy. Once your knife reaches the cutting board, tilt your knife to the right and leave the pieces there. Continue cutting until you reach the far left of the saku.

Use a spoon to scrape the tuna flesh off the reserved skin to use for poke bowls and *negitoro* (see Crispy Toro Hand Roll, page 125). If any sinews come off with the flesh, carefully scrape the flesh from the sinews and discard the sinews.

02

Cutting Toro

01 Taking off the top triangle, or "tempa"; this block will cost about $2,000.

02 Cut into the sinew at a 90-degree angle to minimize sinew separation.

03 Toro saku coming off.

If you have a fatty portion (*toro*) of tuna, the meat will have a tendency to separate a bit from each sinew. While belly-side toro offers robust richness in flavor (and is more costly than the back side toro), toro from the back side has a smoother texture and is more subtle in flavor. My wife and I prefer toro from the back side for this reason. Plus, it is easier to slice than the belly side.

03

FLATFISH (FLUKE, FLOUNDER, AND HALIBUT)

We use smaller flatfish such as fluke, small halibut, and flounder for sushi. They need to be filleted differently than round fish, like sea bass and red snapper. Make sure any flatfish you intend to eat raw was flash frozen to kill any potential parasites.

Cutting Flatfish

Because most small fish sinews are shaped like a "V," you don't need to worry about the angle at which to start cutting against the sinews. Simply place the thicker side of the saku/fillet away from you. Cut it parallel when the sinews have the same distance from each other.

Once you are closer to the tail of the fillet, the distance between each sinew will be different (getting smaller as you get closer to the tail). In that case, cut slices to create a "folding fan" or letter "W," rather than rectangular shapes. Scraps can be used for poke, chopped for hand rolls, or used in ceviche for lean white-fleshed fish.

Note: Another cutting technique often used for flatfish sashimi is called sogi kiri. You can read more about it on page 144.

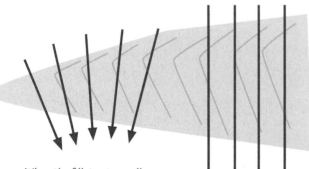

When the fillet gets smaller, cut at an angle.

Make parallel cuts that are the same width apart.

BEHIND THE SCENES MATTERS

Chef Kazunori Nozawa, founder of the famous Sugarfish chain in Los Angeles and New York City, started his day early.

Before his restaurant, Sushi Nozawa, opened each day, he had already spent four hours prepping and cutting fish after a 5 a.m. fish market run. His restaurant didn't appear fancy, but, behind the scenes, hours of work went into it. Lots of Hollywood heavy hitters were regulars, and some were admonished by him for not eating sushi the way he wanted them to—right away—or for using too much wasabi.

One time, I told him people complained that he didn't smile, didn't know anything about customer service, and that his place looked like a cheap Chinese take-out. His response? No one cared more about the customer than he because of the hours he spent preparing the fish to make sure his customers got the best-tasting sushi. He dedicated his time to customer service before the customers even showed up at the restaurant.

SALMON

Salmon is usually sold in fillet form, as bone-in steaks, or "portions" that are halved and boneless. Salmon fillets are easiest to work with, but if you buy a whole fish, you'll have to fillet it yourself. Be especially careful to make sure your salmon comes from a trusted source and has been flash frozen to kill any parasites.

Filleting Salmon and Preparing the Fillets

01 Remove the scales. Cut off the head off, gills, and collar bones. Hold the Santoku hocho in your dominant hand, and with the other, hold the fish.

02 Insert your hocho into the dorsal fin side near the head end and slice toward the tail.

03 Once you reach the tail, start slicing back toward the head end. Place the fillet off to the side and then repeat the above steps to remove the backbone. Try to leave as little meat on the bone as possible.

04 Next, slice off the thin, white, paper-like membranes and cut the belly flaps off of each fillet—from the soft, white skin to about 1 inch (2.5 cm) from where the backbone was. (Sear these up later and roll them into a handroll with sushi rice and chopped onions.) Then, using a tweezer, remove all pin bones, which are within the flesh. Finally, to remove the skin, place the salmon, skin-side down, on a cutting board and hold your knife parallel to it. While pulling the knife toward you, carefully slice the salmon off the skin as closely as possible. Reserve the skin for salmon skin rolls or salad.

Cutting Salmon Portions into Saku Strips

Japanese and some Korean groceries typically sell pre-cut saku strips. If you don't have access to these, go to a reputable seafood market (see Resources, page 163) and ask them to cut a salmon portion 7 to 8 inches (18 to 20 cm) in length parallel to the backbone, with the backbone and pin bones removed. Then:

05 Halve the salmon portion by sliding your knife where the backbone used to be.

06 Cut each side in half in the same direction as your first cut.

07 Now you have four saku strips.

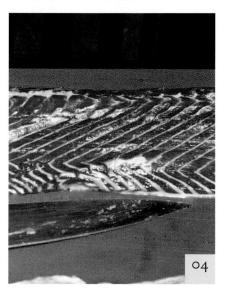

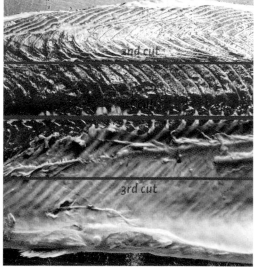

2nd cut

1st cut

3rd cut

Slicing a Salmon Saku Strip for Sushi/Sashimi

Place the wider side of the fillet away from you, skin-side (looks gray after you peeled off the skin) down.

For nigiri, holding your knife at a 45-degree angle, cut the salmon against the sinews (the white bands) into $1/4$-inch (0.6 cm) slices.

For sushi rolls, slice the fillet along its length into $1/2$-inch (1 cm) strips, about $2 1/2$ inches (6 cm) long. When the fillet gets very small, close to the tail, hold your knife at a 50- to 60-degree angle so the sashimi portions are large enough.

Use a spoon to scrape any flesh from the skin and use it for poke or a Salmon Avocado Rice Bowl (page 74).

Salmon for nigiri. Please note, you should remove the skin from the salmon while filleting. In this book, we kept the skin on to help visualize how the fish is being used.

UNI

To remove the edible part of a live uni, flip the sea urchin over to expose its mouth—you'll see white teeth in the center surrounded by a fleshy ring. With a pair of sharp shears, cut the bottom shell off, snipping around the edge of the shell until the entire innards are exposed. Carefully scoop out the mouth (most of the digestive tract will come with it). Dump out the liquid left in the shell and remove and discard any dark bits (digestive tract), carefully avoiding the brightly colored gonads. You will be left with five gonad lobes.

Carefully rinse the sea urchin. With a spoon, carefully scoop out each lobe and place briefly, just for a couple minutes, in a cold saltwater bath to eliminate undesirable particles, undissolved sea kelp the uni consumed, etc. It's best to use the seawater from the area where the uni was harvested, and do not soak for too long or the flavor will be lost in the saltwater.

The lobes are now ready to eat. This fresh uni won't be as creamy or sweet as commercially prepared uni. All uni recipes in this book use commercially prepared uni, which is my preference.

Uni from Hokkaido

RECIPES

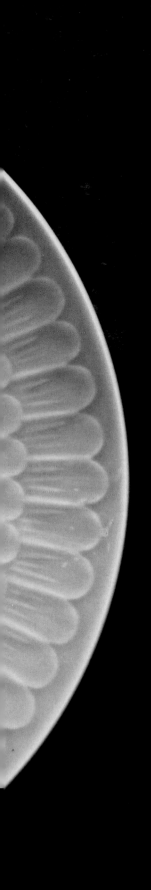

02

Sushi chefs make sushi. Noodle chefs make only noodles. Tempura chefs make one thing—tempura. This is the way it works at professional-level restaurants in Japan. When you go to Japan, the good sushi place serves only sushi. The chefs there have dedicated their lives to making just one thing. That's not easy. That's one reason we respect them.

The chefs featured here who generously shared their recipes have been mastering their skills for decades, and some nuances of their dishes might not appear in your re-creations from the start. Yet, the basic components and instructions are here for you to benefit from their years of training. Each of us has a different palate and, therefore, I encourage you to add your own

spin to the flavors created by the masters in this book, thinking especially about the principles of sustainability outlined in the Appendix (see page 160). For example, in the recipe for spicy tuna roll, the chef recommends using sriracha. However, if you like a subtle sweetness behind the spiciness, you could substitute kochujang sauce (Korean sweet and spicy paste, which works well with white-fleshed fish and chicken dishes). For an advanced technique, marinate, or zuke in Japanese, for less time than the chef recommends to achieve a dish more subtly flavored.

Once you learn the basics, play with the recipes to your liking. After all, that's the fun of cooking. I should note that all the chefs' recipes have been adapted to make them more easily understood by home cooks.

RICE

—————

Rice is the staple carb for Japanese people. The rice farm is a centerpiece of "Satoyama" scenery, which represents a coexistence of people and nature in their local village. In Japan, rice was also used for centuries as a form of currency.

When a Japanese chef prepares fish, the chef first cuts the sashimi or nigiri portions. Smaller pieces and oddly shaped pieces are used for rolls. Respected chefs in Japan don't let anything go to the trash bin, and they take pride in that. They can make fish chips out of fish skin; fish bones and fins, of course, make soup stock. Certainly we (myself included) are not skilled enough or have the time to do all those things, but we can at least make rice bowls and pokes—save fish while saving money!

When the U.S. government started enriching white rice with B vitamins and other nutrients, consumers were advised not to wash the rice because it would rinse away the nutrients. But the washing and rinsing steps are critical to producing properly cooked Japanese-style rice. You may find your rice comes out better if you perform step 1 as written here. But the choice is totally up to you.

Steamed Japanese-Style Rice

INGREDIENTS

2 cups (370 g) Japanese short-grain white rice

2¼ cups (540 ml) water

Makes 4 cups (800 g)

STEPS

1 **Place a large bowl in the sink and pour the rice into it. Fill the bowl with enough cold water to cover the rice generously. With your hand, swish the rice around until the water becomes cloudy. Drain the rice in a fine-mesh sieve. Repeat this step three or four times more until the water being poured off is almost clear. Drain well.**

2 **Transfer the rice to a rice cooker or a medium saucepan. Add the water and cover the pan. Turn on the rice cooker, or bring the water to a boil over high heat. Reduce the heat to low and cook the rice cook until the water has been absorbed, 18 to 20 minutes. Remove the pan from the heat and let sit, still covered, for 10 minutes.**

Note: If using brown rice, use an additional ½ cup (120 ml) of water to cook and allow 20 minutes total for cooking time.

Sushi Rice

Sushi rice is not just plain steamed rice. It may look like it, but it's actually seasoned with vinegar. In fact, master sushi chefs, such as Jiro Sukiyabashi, who served President Obama, use two or three different versions of sushi rice each day. Sometimes their sushi rice is pure white and sometimes it has a reddish tone, depending on the vinegar used for seasoning. Chefs use different vinegars for different fish, just as you might use robustly flavored olive oil for certain dishes and subtly mannered olive oil for others. Brown rice is not common for sushi, but I will include it in this book, as it is becoming more popular.

INGREDIENTS

2 cups (370 g) Japanese short-grain white or brown rice

2¼ cups (540 ml) water (if using white rice), or 2¾ cups (660 ml) water (for brown rice)

½ cup (120 ml) rice vinegar

1 tablespoon (12.5 g) sugar

1 tablespoon (18 g) sea salt

Makes 4 cups (800 g)

STEPS

1 Place a large bowl in the sink and pour the rice into it. Add enough cold water to cover the rice generously. With your hand, swish the rice around until the water becomes cloudy. Drain the rice in a fine-mesh sieve. Repeat this step three or four times more until the water being poured off is almost clear. Drain well.

2 Transfer the rice to a rice cooker or a medium saucepan. Add the water and cover the pan. Turn on the rice cooker, or bring the water to a boil over high heat. Reduce the heat to low and cook the rice until the water has been absorbed, 18 to 20 minutes for white rice and double that for brown rice. Remove the pan from the heat and let sit, still covered, for 10 minutes.

3 While the rice cooks, prepare the sushi vinegar (*sushi-zu*). In a small bowl, stir together the vinegar, sugar, and salt until the sugar and salt dissolve. Set aside.

4 Spread the rice into a bed in a shallow bowl. Pour the sushi vinegar over the rice. You may want to use a *shamoji*, or rice scoop, to more evenly distribute the vinegar. Mix it well without pressing too hard. Try to keep the rice fluffy and moist. Cover the bowl with a wet cloth until you are ready to make the sushi. The rice should be served at room temperature.

Note: Today you have the option of making sushi rice with brown rice. Many sushi bars in Los Angeles and San Francisco offer a brown rice option. At K-Zo in Culver City, California, chef-owner Keizo Ishiba will make all your omakase sushi with brown rice, and the rice balls keep their shape. The reason they hold together, he says, is thanks to a good rice vinegar.

There are literally hundreds of bowls around with an infinite number of combinations of grains, vegetables, meats, and seafood. The basic guideline for a rice bowl is something laid over rice, so you, too, can create your own easily. Because we are talking about fish in this book, I'll introduce one with the fish that most of us are very familiar with—yes, salmon. Accessible, tasty, and not that expensive, salmon, together with avocado, makes a visually appealing dish.

Salmon Avocado Rice Bowl

INGREDIENTS

Sauce

2 tablespoons (30 ml) soy sauce

1 tablespoon (15 ml) mirin

1 teaspoon (5 ml) sesame oil

Scant 1 to 1½ tablespoons (5 to 10 g) wasabi powder (depending on how spicy you want it), mixed with water to form a paste

Rice Bowl

3½ ounces (100 g) sashimi-grade skinless salmon fillet, cut into ⅔-inch (1.5 cm) cubes

1 avocado, pitted, peeled, and cut into ⅔-inch (1.5 cm) cubes

2 cups (400 g) Steamed Japanese-Style (white or brown) Rice (page 71)

2 cherry tomatoes, quartered

Pinch *kizami nori* (shredded nori)

One 2-inch (5 cm) length scallion, trimmed to remove the last ½ inch (1 cm) of the white end, chopped

Serves 2

STEPS

1 **To make the sauce: In a medium bowl, stir together the soy sauce, mirin, sesame oil, and wasabi paste. Set aside.**

2 **To make the rice bowl: Add the salmon and avocado cubes to the sauce and let marinate for 15 minutes.**

3 **Using a *shamoji* (rice scoop), spoon the rice into serving bowls and top with the salmon and avocado mixture, plus the sauce.**

4 **Garnish with the tomatoes. Sprinkle the kizami nori and scallion over the top just before serving.**

A classic snack of leftover rice steeped in water, broth, or dashi, ochazuke can be a bowl of comfort when you add leftover grilled salmon and vegetables. I make this with clams when I have had too much to drink the night before. Adding wasabi gives the soup a zip.

Ochazuke with Grilled Salmon Flakes

INGREDIENTS

2½ cups (600 ml) Dashi (page 153)

1 tablespoon (15 ml) soy sauce

2 teaspoons (10 ml) mirin

Scant 1 tablespoon (5 g) kombucha tea powder

2 pinches sea salt

1½ cups (300 g) Steamed Japanese-Style Rice (page 71), freshly steamed or left over

Leftover cooked salmon, as much or as little as you have or like, deboned

Pinch *kizami nori* (shredded nori)

3 to 4 whole stems mizuna (Japanese mustard greens), or fresh cilantro

Wasabi powder mixed with water to form a paste, to taste

Serves 2

STEPS

1 In a medium saucepan over medium heat, combine the dashi, soy sauce, mirin, kombucha powder, and salt. Bring to a simmer.

2 Using a *shamoji* (rice scoop), spoon the rice into serving bowls. Flake the salmon (make sure all the small bones have been removed) over the rice.

3 Top the rice with the kizami nori, mizuna, and wasabi.

4 Pour the hot dashi broth over the rice and serve.

MASTER VARIATION
CHEF DAVIN WAITE |
WRENCH AND RODENT SEABASSTROPUB |
San Diego, CA

Instead of using kaiware sprouts and avocado, Chef Davin topped this Ahi Poke Bowl with ogo nori, pickled carrot, and heirloom purple carrots, which taste just like a carrot but with a touch of beet flavor.

Ahi Poke Bowl

Poke has become enormously popular in the last five years, so most people know what a poke bowl is: a base—typically rice—cubed raw sashimi-grade fish (typically salmon, tuna, albacore tuna, or hamachi), and Asian toppings such as seaweed and furikake sprinkles. In Hawaii, some stores offer 72 types of pokes, including squid, shrimp, scallops, and swordfish. We will make a basic ahi poke here. You can find Chef Davin Waite's Master Variation of the dish as shown in the photo in its accompanying box. Ahi means "tuna" in the Hawaiian language, so ahi tuna steak on a menu literally means "tuna tuna steak," which sounds funny to me.

INGREDIENTS

Sauce

2 tablespoons (30 ml) soy sauce

1 tablespoon (15 ml) sesame oil

1 teaspoon (5 ml) mirin

1 teaspoon (2.7 g) grated peeled fresh ginger (*shoga*)

1 teaspoon (2.7 g) white or black sesame seeds, toasted

Bowl

¼ onion, thinly sliced

¼ (2½-ounce, or 70 g) package kaiware (daikon radish) sprouts

7 ounces (200 g) sashimi-grade tuna loin, cut into ⅔-inch (1.5 cm) cubes

½ avocado, peeled, pitted, and cut into ⅔-inch (1.5 cm) cubes

2½ to 3 cups (500 to 600 g) Steamed Japanese-Style Rice (page 71)

Pinch *kizami nori* (shredded nori)

Serves 3 or 4

STEPS

1 **To make the sauce:** In a medium bowl, stir together the soy sauce, sesame oil, mirin, ginger, and sesame seeds. Measure 1 tablespoon (15 ml) and set aside.

2 **To make the bowl:** Rinse the onion with water to soften its bitterness. Drain well. Cut off the roots of the radish sprouts and cut the sprouts about ¾ inch (2 cm) long.

3 To the sauce, add the tuna, avocado, and onion and gently stir to combine.

4 Using a *shamoji* (rice scoop), spoon the rice into serving bowls. Top the rice with the tuna mixture and sauce. Sprinkle the kizami nori on top. Pour the reserved 1 tablespoon (15 ml) of sauce over the seaweed and garnish with the radish sprouts for crunch.

Note: Unfortunately, most poke bowls I've tried in the mainland United States weren't as good as those in Hawaii. Why? Because they use carbon monoxide–treated tuna in the mainland, whereas Hawaiians use only freshly caught tuna. Carbon monoxide is injected with tiny needles to turn the tuna flesh from a brown color to bright red. Once injected, the tuna flesh remains artificially pinkish red and/or fluorescent red for 2 weeks after it is thawed, making it extremely hard to tell how old the tuna is. Consumers have become seriously ill in Japan, Canada, and Europe, so CO-treated tuna is banned in those countries. Here, I ask you to source "non-artificially colored" tuna. These natural fish might not be perfectly red, but if sourced from a place I recommend (see page 163), you are in good hands in terms of quality and responsible harvesting.

Sake Onigiri
Salmon Rice Balls

Onigiri, or rice balls, are soul food for the Japanese. Going back to the eleventh century, samurai soldiers ate onigiri before battles. Since the fifteenth century, Japanese travelers have carried onigiri on long walking journeys. My mother used to make this onigiri for me when I went on school field trips, and my father and I would carry several onigiri when we went fishing on weekends. The butter adds a slight flavor that pairs well with the salt while also helping prevent the rice from sticking to your hands.

Onigiri also has a sustainable character. You can throw in leftovers, such as fish, chicken, and vegetables—which I'm sure my mother did, as smart as she is. Because it is so easy and fun to make, onigiri is also a nice way for a family to prepare a meal together.

INGREDIENTS

Scant ¾ ounce (20 g) broiled salmon, flaked

1½ tablespoons (27 g) sea salt

2 teaspoons (10 g) butter

2 to 3 cups (400 to 600 g) Steamed Japanese-Style Rice (page 71) or Sushi Rice (page 72)

2 sheets nori, halved

Serves 2

STEPS

1 **In a large bowl, stir together the salmon flakes, salt, butter, and rice.**

2 **Wet your hands with water (to avoid having the rice stick to your hands) and form half the mixture into a ball, or any shape you like.**

3 **Use the nori sheet like a tortilla, to hold the onigiri without your fingers touching the sticky rice.**

4 **Repeat to make the second onigiri. Serve immediately so the nori stays nice and crisp.**

Sake onigiri come in many shapes and sizes, so get creative! Here, Chef Davin Waite rolls them into convenient triangle handrolls.

APPETIZERS

Sushi chefs like their menus to reflect what's in season—both fish and vegetables—in everything they serve, including appetizers. As with soups (see page 148), appetizers are a good way to utilize leftover fish. Often, smaller portions of fish not big enough to make it as sashimi or nigiri become appetizers prepared with different cooking methods and sauces.

From salty pickles to spicy peppers and smoked salmon, the food that comes out before the meal should make you hungrier for more. As with sushi, these appetizers are about texture and flavor, as well as being a feast for the eyes.

Seared Albacore Tuna Salad

CHEF KEN NAMBA | KIRIKO SUSHI |
Los Angeles, CA

Albacore tuna is a very versatile fish for cooking. It is good for sashimi and sushi, and works well with ponzu sauce, soy sauce, sesame seed dressing, or miso dressing. It is also a sustainable alternative to other tuna species that have been overfished by the "purse seiner" method (for canned tuna, see page 34) in some parts of the ocean.

Albacore tuna flesh is soft and pink, compared to the red color found in the flesh of other larger tuna species. During cold-water months, some get very fatty and you can get great toro from them. Albacore tuna toro melts in your mouth, with no tough sinew to get in the way of its smooth texture.

INGREDIENTS

1 teaspoon (5 ml) grapeseed oil

About 1 pound (400 to 500 g) albacore tuna loins, fresh or frozen

2 tablespoons (30 ml) Ponzu Sauce (page 159)

1 tablespoon (15 ml) soy sauce

1 tablespoon (15 ml) sesame oil

1 tablespoon (15 ml) cooking-grade sake

1-inch (2.5 cm) piece fresh ginger (*shoga*), peeled and finely grated

4 cups (284 g) mixed salad greens

¼ carrot, thinly sliced

Small bunch *kaiware* (daikon radish sprouts)

2 radishes, thinly sliced

8 fresh chives, chopped

Serves 4

STEPS

1 **In a skillet over high heat, heat the grapeseed oil. Add the tuna and sear each side for just a few seconds until the surface changes color to beige. Remove from the skillet and thinly slice the tuna against the grain.**

2 **In a small bowl, whisk the ponzu sauce, soy sauce, sesame oil, sake, and ginger until well blended. Set aside.**

3 **In a large bowl or on a serving platter, toss together the greens, carrots, kaiware, radishes, and chives.**

4 **Arrange the seared albacore tuna slices on the salad. Pour the dressing over the salad and serve.**

Note: Vary the dressing: Use a miso-ginger dressing, a sesame seed–based ginger dressing, or even an olive oil and balsamic vinegar dressing. Yellowfin tuna can replace the albacore, especially a small one (with a loin under 6 pounds, or 2.7 kg, in size). You can tell the size of the tuna (or other large fish) when it's in loin form by looking at the distance between the sinews when the flesh is cut at a 90-degree angle from the cutting board. If the tuna is big, the sinews will be ½ inch (1 cm) apart. If the tuna is small, the distance will be less than that. The bigger ones have a tendency to taste strongly of iron and acid. Small ones have almost no flavor so they go well with the dressing, but some might be missing the tuna flavor.

To preserve vegetables, many cultures have their own versions of pickles, such as sauerkraut in the West or Korean kimchi. In Japan, each prefecture has its own version of tsukemono utilizing local veggies. This recipe is for a very basic pickle that will appeal to many. You can replace the cucumber with daikon radish, cabbage, and so on. You can even add different flavors to the pickling liquid, such as wasabi or miso—the variations are endless.

Tsukemono *Japanese Pickles*

INGREDIENTS

4 Japanese cucumbers, peeled

1 red bell pepper, stemmed, seeded, and cut into rings (or daikon radish, eggplant, carrot, or any other vegetable you'd like to pickle)

3 tablespoons plus 1 teaspoon (50 ml total) Dashi (page 153)

Scant ½ teaspoon (3 g) sea salt

Serves 4

STEPS

1 **Cut each cucumber into 4 even pieces for a total of 16 pieces.**

2 **In a large resealable plastic bag, combine the cucumbers, red bell pepper, dashi, and salt. Seal the bag. Make sure all the ingredients are mixed evenly by massaging the cucumbers from the outside of the bag with your hands for 15 seconds. Let the cucumber soak in the liquid for at least 30 minutes before eating. For longer soaking times, place the bag in the refrigerator.**

Shishito Peppers

CHEF HIRO OBAYASHI | *Portland, OR*

Shishito peppers have become very popular in recent years, I think because they are one of the basic items at izakaya restaurants (Japanese tapas bars with charcoal grills). This is fun to serve— while most shishito peppers aren't hot, some, perhaps one out of ten, are very spicy. Jalapeño spicy! You can't tell by looking at them, so you take the risk when eating.

Another thing I like about this appetizer is that it maintains its flavor when reheated the next day. The only problem when reviving this dish is the dry bonito flakes won't be crisp, so you might have to sprinkle on more. Other than that, this dish is resilient against time.

INGREDIENTS

5 to 10 shishito peppers, stemmed

2 tablespoons (30 ml) vegetable oil

Pinch sea salt

Pinch freshly ground black pepper

Bonito flakes, to taste, for serving

Serves 2

STEPS

1   **Cut a ½-inch (1 cm) slit at the tip of each pepper.**

2   **In a skillet over high heat, heat the vegetable oil. Add the peppers and turn the heat to medium. Sauté the peppers until browned but not mushy.**

3   **Sprinkle with the salt, pepper, and bonito flakes and serve.**

Asparagus Goma-Ae

Sesame Asparagus

CHEF HIRO OBAYASHI | Portland, OR

Goma, in Japanese, means toasted sesame seeds. Ae means, "mix with dressing," just as you mix dressing for a Caesar salad. Asparagus gives texture and the goma lends a savory scent and subtle sweetness. Vinegar stimulates your palate. This dish maintains its flavor well when refrigerated, if you would like to make it ahead.

For a well-balanced, healthy, and sustainable meal for cold nights, serve this dish as an appetizer, followed by warm Ara Jiru (page 155), and finish with Sake Onigiri (page 78) with chunks of grilled fish meat inside. On hot summer days, serve cold Corn Soup (page 157) instead. Roll onigiri with cold pickled cucumber or radish inside the rice balls.

INGREDIENTS

Sauce

1 cup (144 g) sesame seeds, toasted, plus some for garnish

½ cup (120 ml) Dashi (page 153)

½ cup (120 ml) soy sauce

½ cup (120 ml) cooking-grade sake (see Tip)

⅓ cup (67 g) sugar

2 pounds (908 g) asparagus, tough ends trimmed

Pinch sea salt

Serves 4

STEPS

1   Prepare a large bowl of ice water and set aside.

2   In a food processor, combine the sesame seeds, dashi, soy sauce, sake, and sugar. Process until well blended. Set the sauce aside.

3   Bring a large pot of water to a boil over high heat. Add the asparagus and salt. Boil the asparagus for about 3 minutes, or until it reaches the desired tenderness. Drain and transfer the asparagus to the ice water to stop the cooking. Drain thoroughly.

4   Arrange the asparagus on a serving platter, pour the dressing over, garnish with sesame seeds, and serve.

Tip: Instead of using sake and sugar in the sauce, use ½ cup (120 ml) mirin. And feel free to add different flavors as you like, such as mango sauce to give it a taste of the tropics. You can also use white asparagus for a different look.

Kanpachi Carpaccio with Tosazu Gelée

CHEF KEN NAMBA | KIRIKO SUSHI |
Los Angeles, CA

You often see hamachi (farmed yellowtail from Japan) carpaccio on the menu at sushi bars and high-end seafood restaurants. So let's make an appetizer one notch up. Kanpachi (farmed amberjack) is very similar to hamachi; however, it has a firmer texture and tastes cleaner. Hamachi is very rich in oil whereas kanpachi is less so, which enables you to taste the flavor of the fish. (Oily doesn't mean tasty. Tasting its oil and tasting its flavor are two different things.)

This appetizer is easy to make and you can add your own spin by using a different fish, or adding different ingredients, such as sriracha, for spiciness, or use a different oil, like sesame oil, and so on.

INGREDIENTS

Tosazu

1¼ cups (300 ml) filtered water

¾ cup plus 4 teaspoons (200 ml) rice vinegar

6 tablespoons plus 2 teaspoons (100 ml) mirin

6 tablespoons plus 2 teaspoons (100 ml) *usukuchi* (lighter colored) soy sauce

About 1 heaping cup (10 g) *katsuobushi* (dried bonito flakes)

Juice of 1 lemon

Tosazu Gelée

1 cup plus 2 teaspoons (250 ml) tosazu (recipe above)

2 teaspoons (5 g) powdered gelatin

2 teaspoons (10 ml) freshly squeezed lemon juice

Scant 2 teaspoons (5 g) yuzu pepper

Shiso Paste

¾ cup plus 4 teaspoons (200 ml) extra-virgin olive oil

10 fresh shiso leaves

2 teaspoons (5 g) pine nuts

1 clove garlic, grated

Scant ½ teaspoon (2.5 g) sea salt

Kanpachi

8 ounces (225 g) sashimi-grade kanpachi, sliced sashimi size (½ ounce, or 15 to 17 g each)

1 jalapeño pepper, thinly sliced

Scant ¼ cup (5 g) rainbow mix microgreens

Sea salt (optional)

Freshly squeezed lemon juice, for seasoning (optional)

Extra-virgin olive oil, for drizzling (optional)

Serves 4 to 6

STEPS

────────

1 To make the tosazu: In a medium saucepan over medium-high heat, combine all the ingredients except the katsuobushi and lemon. Bring to a boil, but just before reaching the boiling point, add the bonito flakes and lemon. Let cool to room temperature (not refrigerated).

2 Line a fine-mesh sieve with cheesecloth and place it over a bowl. Pour the sauce through to filter it. Transfer to an airtight container and keep refrigerated for up to 3 weeks.

3 To make the tosazu gelée: In a small saucepan over medium-high heat, stir together the tosazu and gelatin. Cook until just before it boils and remove from the heat. Transfer to a small bowl, cover, and refrigerate.

4 Once solidified, run lukewarm water over the bowl for a few seconds (this helps release the gelée cleanly from the bowl), remove the gelée, and place it on a cutting board. Using your hocho (knife), chop the gelée into tiny pieces.

5 In the same bowl, stir together the lemon juice and yuzu pepper. Add the gelée pieces back into the bowl. If you do it quickly, it sparkles more.

6 To make and shiso paste: In a food processor (do not use a Vitamix; it will process the ingredients too finely), combine all the paste ingredients and process until blended.

7 To make the kanpachi: On a round plate, arrange the kanpachi pieces in a circle. Spread the tosazu gelée evenly on each sashimi slice and top each with a slice of jalapeño.

8 Arrange the microgreens in the center of the sashimi. Drizzle with the shiso paste. If desired, sprinkle with salt, lemon juice, and/or olive oil.

This smoked salmon may not be what you're used to. The outside is lightly cooked and smoked, but the inside is still sushi salmon. Savor the different textures as you bite into it. The smoked salmon also makes a versatile base for different appetizers—wrap the smoked salmon with mango, dip it in tartar sauce, use it for nigiri, or make salmon tartar with it. It also makes a flavorful sandwich. Once prepared, this sushi smoked salmon will keep in your refrigerator for about 2 days to enjoy. To accomplish the smoking, you will need 4 ounces (115 g) of wood chips.

Sushi Smoked Salmon

CHEF KEN NAMBA | KIRIKO SUSHI |
Los Angeles, CA

INGREDIENTS

10½ ounces (300 g) sashimi-grade fresh salmon fillet with skin and scales on (to prevent shrinkage)

2 tablespoons (25 g) sugar

2 tablespoons plus 1 teaspoon (75 g) rock salt

½ cup (120 ml) olive oil

½ cup (120 ml) canola oil

Serves 4 to 6

STEPS

1 **To prepare the fish, remove all the pin bones with tweezers (or buy fillets with pin bones already removed). Cut off the belly flap, if it comes with the fillet portion, and save it to use in another dish. Lay the fillet, skin-side down, on a tray. In a small bowl, combine the sugar and rock salt and cover the fillet with it. Let sit for 4 to 5 hours at room temperature; the sugar and salt will "cook" the surface of the fish.**

2 **Lightly wash the salt/sugar mixture from the fillet and put the fillet in the freezer for 30 to 60 minutes—freezing the surface is important to help keep the inside somewhat raw so it does not cook all the way through! The fillet should feel frozen when you touch it.**

3 **Put the wood chips in the bottom of a roasting pan. Remove the fillet from the freezer and place the meat, skin-side down, on a metal rack that fits inside the roasting pan. Tightly cover the pan with aluminum foil and place the pan on the stove over medium heat. Once you see smoke coming from the pan, continue to heat for just 15 seconds more. Then turn off the heat, but leave the pan covered for 5 to 7 minutes more so the outer crust is smoked and cooked while the inside is still sashimi.**

4 **In a medium bowl, stir together the olive oil and canola oil. Paint the surface of the fish with the oil mixture. Use immediately or wrap tightly in plastic wrap and keep refrigerated for 2 to 3 days.**

MASTER VARIATION
CHEF MASAYUKI FURUKAWA |
MASA SUSHI |
Kumegawa, Tokyo, Japan

———

Traditionally, raw ankimo is formed
into a cylinder, wrapped in cheesecloth,
and steamed. Here, Chef Masayuki
Furukawa cuts the cooked ankimo
cylinder in half lengthwise and then
into 1-inch (2.5 cm) slices before serving
it with a daikon-ponzu sauce, red
pepper paste, and scallions.

Ankimo, or monkfish liver, is a healthier and more humane alternative to foie gras because you don't have to push feed down the throat of a monkfish. Monkfish can swim all over the ocean with their unique "lantern" light so they can catch food in pitch black, deep on the ocean bottom. The base color of an ankimo is a peachy cream color; those with lots of large orange spots on the surface and inside are the tasty ones. It is a good choice to use in onigiri. This recipe is for a soup version, but for a more traditional preparation, see Chef Masayuki Furukawa's Master Variation at left.

Ankimo with Dashi Daikon

INGREDIENTS

About 1½ ounces (40 g) fresh ankimo (monkfish liver)

One 8-inch (20 cm) daikon radish, cut into ½-inch (1-cm) cubes

1⅓ cups (320 ml) Dashi (page 153)

2 tablespoons plus 2 teaspoons (40 ml) *usukuchi* (light) soy sauce

2 tablespoons plus 2 teaspoons (40 ml) mirin

2 tablespoons plus 2 teaspoons (40 ml) cooking-grade sake

Serves 4

STEPS

1 Slice the ankimo into 4 pieces, 2 inches (5 cm) in diameter and ½ inch (1 cm) in thickness. Leave under a trickling stream of running water for 1 hour to remove all traces of blood.

Tip: If you see any worms in the ankimo, remove them with tweezers.

2 Meanwhile, place the daikon in a saucepan, cover with water, and boil for 20 minutes. Drain well and return the daikon to the pan.

3 Return the saucepan to high heat and add the dashi, soy sauce, mirin, and sake. Bring to a boil. Add the ankimo and boil for 20 minutes. Remove from the heat and let sit so the flavor can soak into both the daikon and the ankimo.

Tip: Double boiling the daikon will soften it enough so the texture between the daikon and ankimo is different, but not so different, when consumed together.

4 Serve warm in a bowl with the cooking liquid, which helps cut the richness of the fish, or chill everything in the refrigerator before serving—either way is good. I recommend eating a small bite of ankimo and daikon together; the dashi bridges the flavors nicely.

Nothing says summer better than tasty heirloom tomatoes and mild white-fleshed fish—and, every summer, a tomato plant just happens to overtake the planter on our back patio herb garden. We love using different parts of the same plant to layer flavors and showcase delicious parts of plants not typically eaten, like tomato leaves. This dish is best enjoyed cool on a warm summer day.

Fluke with Garden Tomato Salsa

CHEF DAVIN WAITE | WRENCH AND RODENT SEABASSTROPUB | *San Diego, CA*

INGREDIENTS

Salsa

2 cups (360 g) diced tomatoes, preferably organic heirloom

1 teaspoon (6 g) sea salt

1 teaspoon (2 g) freshly ground black pepper

¼ cup (60 ml) freshly squeezed tangerine juice

2 teaspoons (10 ml) fish sauce, or 2 tablespoons (30 ml) Dashi (page 153)

¼ cup (40 g) thinly sliced red onion, rinsed

2 teaspoons (6 g) finely minced garlic

Fish

8 ounces (225 g) boneless, skinless fillet of fluke, halibut, or other mild white-fleshed fish

2 tablespoons (30 ml) extra-virgin olive oil

12 fresh tomato leaves

Serves 4

STEPS

1 **To make the salsa: Put the tomatoes in a medium bowl, sprinkle with the salt and pepper, and let sit at room temperature for 10 minutes until the salt pulls the juices from the tomatoes.**

2 **Add the tangerine juice and fish sauce. Toss in the onion and garlic. Refrigerate for 20 minutes.**

3 **To plate the fish: Slice the fish as thinly as possible and arrange on a serving plate. Using a slotted spoon, scoop the salsa onto the plate. Drizzle the fish with some of the remaining salsa juices, drip the olive oil sparingly around the plate, arrange the tomato leaves on top, and serve.**

Note: Purslane makes a great substitute for tomato leaves. To take the dish in a different direction, replace the tomato leaves with basil or flat-leaf parsley.

Yellowtail with Beet Green Relish

CHEF DAVIN WAITE | WRENCH AND RODENT
SEABASSTROPUB | *San Diego, CA*

Some of the best flavors in a plant hide in the lesser-used parts. This dish is a prime example of how a beet's stems and leaves can be used to highlight the vibrancy of mid-size amberjack, wild yellowtail, kampachi (greater amberjack), or hiramasa (Pacific yellowtail), depending on what you have in season and locally available.

Many of you will read this book in different parts of the world. Rather than trying to use ingredients not at their best or not readily available, have some fun, embrace your surroundings, experiment, and make this recipe your own! Think of these recipes as fluid formulas rather than rigid rules. The ingredients for this recipe are based on what is available in Oceanside, California. Substitute seasonal, local ingredients whenever possible—your taste buds will thank you!

INGREDIENTS

Beet Green Relish

1 tablespoon (15 ml) extra-virgin olive oil

1 cup (160 g) diced onion

4 cups (160 g) finely chopped red beet stems and greens

1 teaspoon (6 g) sea salt, plus more to taste

1 teaspoon (2 g) freshly ground black pepper

1 cup (240 ml) *sushi-zu* (see Note)

Yellowtail

3½ ounces (100 g) sashimi-grade yellowtail

Tangerine Oil (see recipe at right)

Fresh cilantro or parsley leaves, for garnish

Sea salt

Serves 4

STEPS

1 **To make the beet green relish: In a medium saucepan over high heat, heat the olive oil until it shimmers. Add the onion, turn the heat to medium, and sauté until it is softened, about 3 minutes.**

2 **Add the beet greens and stems, salt, and pepper. Sauté for 2 to 3 minutes more until the greens are wilted. Add the sushi-zu, lower the heat to a simmer, stir well, and simmer for 1 minute.**

3 **Let cool, then refrigerate for about 2 hours.**

4 **To plate the fish: Cut the yellowtail into 20 sashimi slices and arrange on a plate. Place 1 heaping tablespoon (15 g) of beet relish next to each piece of fish. Drizzle with the remaining liquid. Dot with tangerine oil and garnish with cilantro. Finish with a sprinkling of sea salt.**

Notes: To make an earthier yellow relish, or to use with a fattier fish, make the relish with golden beets and replace the tangerine oil with lemongrass oil or kefir lime oil.

Sushi-zu is seasoned rice vinegar used to flavor rice—especially for sushi. To make 1 cup (240 ml), combine ½ cup (120 ml) rice vinegar, scant ½ cup (90 g) sugar, and scant 2 tablespoons (30 g) salt.

TANGERINE OIL

Make this oil when tangerines are in season. Other good options, if tangerines are not in season, are Valencia or mandarin oranges.

INGREDIENTS

2 cups (480 ml) olive oil (does not have to be extra virgin)

¼ teaspoon sea salt

¾ cup (75 g) organic tangerine peels

Makes about 2 cups (480 ml)

STEPS

In a blender, combine all the ingredients and process on high speed for 2 minutes. Strain the oil through a fine-mesh sieve, coffee filter, or cheesecloth into a glass jar. Discard the solids. Cover and store at room temperature for up to 3 days.

One of my biggest sources of inspiration when preparing parts of fish not typically consumed in the United States is looking to other cultures—and looking to the past. This dish may seem strange to the American palate, but it has been around in one form or another since humans started eating fish. If you can't get bloodline, ask your fishmonger for meat close to the bloodline, which has concentrated sinews. Boiling it softens the sinews.

Tuna Bloodline Yakitori

CHEF DAVIN WAITE | WRENCH AND RODENT
SEABASSTROPUB | *San Diego, CA*

INGREDIENTS

12 ounces (340 g) tuna bloodline

½ cup (120 ml) soy sauce

½ cup (120 ml) mirin

¼ cup (60 ml) *sushi-zu* (see Note, page 96)

¼ cup packed (60 g) light brown sugar

1 teaspoon (2 g) ground white pepper, plus more to taste

2 teaspoons (6 g) minced garlic

2 teaspoons (6 g) grated peeled fresh ginger (*shoga*)

2 teaspoons (10 ml) olive oil (optional)

Serves 4

STEPS

1 **Cut the bloodline into strips measuring ½ inch by 3 inches (1 cm by 7.5 cm), making sure to cut at a 90-degree angle against the grain of the fish. Place the strips in a bowl under a trickling stream of cold running water for 30 minutes, draining off the cloudy red water occasionally. Place the fish in a clean dry strainer and shake off the excess water.**

2 **While the water runs on the bloodline, make the marinade: In a small bowl, stir together the soy sauce, mirin, sushi-zu, brown sugar, white pepper, garlic, and ginger, stirring until the sugar dissolves.**

3 **Transfer the fish to a resealable plastic bag and pour the marinade over the fish. Seal the bag and refrigerate overnight to marinate. Meanwhile, soak bamboo skewers in beer or water.**

4 **Prepare a hot fire in a charcoal or gas grill. Skewer the marinated bloodline and place the skewers on the hot grill. Cook for 3 to 4 minutes per side. Alternatively, you can pan-fry them in olive oil over high heat for 3 to 4 minutes per side. Serve immediately.**

Tip: For best results, use binchotan charcoal, a type of Japanese "white" charcoal that burns hotter than regular charcoal, with no flame or smoke.

Note: It may not be easy to find tuna with the bloodline attached, as mentioned on page 41. But tuna is a large fish and discarding its bloodline is a waste. When you purchase a portion of tuna, ask that the bloodline be kept in. Bloodline is about 10 percent of loin weight, so to get the 12 ounces (340 g) needed for this recipe, buy 10 pounds (4.5 kg) of fillet. Think that's is a lot of fish for one household? There are so many ways to use it——12 ounces (340 g) for the bloodline, 4 to 5 pounds (1.8 to 2.3 kg) for sushi, 3 to 4 pounds (1.3 to 1.8 kg) for poke, or whatever combination you prefer.

One of my favorite things about salmon candy is it serves as an addition to a luxe salad or fish charcuterie platter just as well as it does a healthy "junk food" replacement for kids' school lunches or a fun snack. I encourage you to buy a whole fish and experiment with the different parts, learning how to utilize each piece to its maximum potential. During this process, you will produce scraps and trimmings and offcuts that are perfect for this recipe. I recommend using salmon or sea trout because its oil content keeps it moist even after we "dry" it.

Salmon Candy

CHEF DAVIN WAITE | WRENCH AND RODENT
SEABASSTROPUB | *San Diego, CA*

INGREDIENTS

1 cup (225 g) packed light brown sugar

2 tablespoons (36 g) sea salt

8 ounces (225 g) salmon trim (see Note), cut to a thickness of 1 inch (2.5 cm) and long enough to not fall through the grill

2 tablespoons (30 ml) whiskey or brandy

Serves 4

STEPS

1 **In a large bowl, stir together the brown sugar and salt until evenly blended. Add the salmon and whiskey and mix so the salmon is coated with the brine mixture. Transfer to a covered container and refrigerate for 24 hours.**

2 **Preheat a smoker to 170°F (77°C).**

3 **Remove the salmon from the marinade and pat dry. Discard the marinade. Place the salmon in the smoker and smoke for 3 hours. Alternatively, if you don't have a smoker or grill, place the salmon on a wire rack set on a rimmed baking sheet and bake in a 170°F (77°C) oven for 3 hours.**

4 **Let cool before eating. Keep leftovers refrigerated in an airtight container for up to 4 days.**

Notes: For best results, smoke with a mixture of apple and mesquite wood chips or pellets.

On the salmon trim, keep the skin intact but remove the pin bones. The fat underneath the skin is the best-tasting part.

Zuke means "to marinate" in Japanese. The zuke method was developed in old Tokyo four hundred years ago to preserve fish, when no refrigeration was available. Just as there is an aging process for beef, this was the "aging" method for fish in Japan. Zuke adds a very different flavor to lean tuna, with the marinade ingredients moving the flavor toward a subtle sweetness.

Tuna Zuke

CHEF MASA SASAKI | SASAKI |
San Francisco, CA

INGREDIENTS

———

2 cups (480 ml) soy sauce

¼ cup (60 ml) cooking-grade sake

¼ cup (60 ml) mirin

Very scant ¼ cup (2 g) *katsuo-bushi* (dried bonito flakes)

10 ounces (280 g) lean tuna, cut into a block (*saku*) or 10 sashimi-size slices

Wasabi or grated fresh ginger (*shoga*), for serving

Serves 3 to 4

STEPS

———

1 **In a small saucepan over medium heat, stir together the soy sauce, sake, and mirin. Cook until just before it comes to a boil and immediately remove from the heat. Add the bonito flakes and let cool at room temperature. Strain the sauce through a fine-mesh strainer to remove the bonito flakes. Cover and refrigerate until needed.**

2 **Transfer the marinade to a large resealable plastic bag and add the whole saku strip. Seal the bag and let marinate for 5 to 10 minutes. If the tuna has been cut for sashimi or nigiri, marinate for only 1 to 2 minutes.**

3 **Remove the fish from the marinade and pat dry with a paper towel. The fish is now ready to serve as nigiri with sushi rice and wasabi or an edamame bean–size pinch of grated ginger. If you have access to *wagarashi* (Japanese mustard), use it instead of wasabi or grated ginger to present zuke tuna in a unique way (reminds me of beef).**

MAKI

Sustainability comes not only from saving fish in the oceans but also from getting the most out of the leftover fish in your kitchen—a simple way is to make *maki*, rolled sushi.

Maki is what most people outside Japan picture when they think of sushi. It is formed with the help of a bamboo mat known as a *makisu*. Maki is generally wrapped in nori (seaweed), but is also occasionally wrapped in soy paper or cucumber. When buying nori, look for high-grade nori—it will reward you with less breakage when you roll it up.

When you roll the nori, start with the nori placed on the makisu, textured-side up. Before you start rolling, make a bowl of vinegared water to dip your hands into by combining 1 cup (240 ml) water with 3 tablespoons (45 ml) rice vinegar. Working with wet hands to spread the sushi rice on the nori helps you spread it without sticking or tearing the nori.

Each maki is typically cut into four or eight pieces. One roll is good as an appetizer; two rolls are good for a kid's lunch.

While different kinds of maki are served with different garnishes, the ones in this book should be served with soy sauce, wasabi, and *gari* (pickled ginger).

BASIC MAKI TECHNIQUE

01 Open a makisu (bamboo rolling mat) and place one sheet of nori on the mat, textured-side up. With wet hands, spread half the rice on the nori, leaving about one-quarter of the sheet uncovered along the top. Add your fillings, including wasabi, sesame seeds, fish, etc.

02 Start rolling the nori away from you. With your finger, wet the edge of the nori.

03 Continue rolling, keeping the makisu as tight as possible and backing if off when needed so that the mat does not get rolled into the maki.

04 When finished rolling, tighten up the roll once more before releasing it from the rolling mat.

05 Cut the maki into 4 to 8 pieces.

THE INSIDE-OUT OPTION

01   Open a makisu (bamboo rolling mat) and place one sheet of nori on the mat, textured-side up. With wet hands, spread half the rice on the nori, leaving about one-quarter of the sheet uncovered along the top. Sprinkle with sesame seeds, if using. See photo 01 at left.

02   Flip the nori over so that the rice Is on the bottom. (You may want to cover your makisu with a piece of plastic wrap beforehand to help prevent the rice from sticking.) Place your ingredients in a line down the center of the nori.

03   Using your makisu, roll the maki with the same rolling technique described in steps 2, 3, and 4 of "Basic Maki Technique." Cut the roll into 4 to 8 pieces.

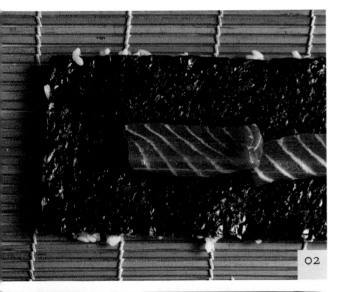

OTHER FUN OPTIONS

You can experiment with your maki by using soy paper (which is white) instead of nori and adding unexpected ingredients inside (photo 01). You can also place ingredients outside of the roll, such as fish scraps, which you can round out with a makisu covered in plastic wrap (photos 02 and 03). The finished result can be really stunning (photo 04).

According to my mother, I started eating this roll at the tender age of two. This is also my son's favorite roll. It represents a great way to eat clean protein and carbs. You can replace tuna with hamachi (farmed Japanese yellowtail) or salmon.

Tekka Maki
Traditional Tuna Roll

INGREDIENTS

———

1 cup (240 ml) water

2 to 3 tablespoons plus 1 teaspoon (35 to 50 ml) rice vinegar

Heaping ½ teaspoon (2.5 g) sugar

Pinch sea salt

About 4 ounces (120 g) warm Steamed Japanese-Style Rice (page 71)

2 sheets nori

Wasabi powder mixed with water to make a paste, for making the rolls and serving

Sesame seeds

½ ounce (15 g) sashimi-grade tuna, cut into sticks about 3½ inches (8.5 cm) long by ½ inch (1 cm) wide

Soy sauce, for serving

Makes 2 rolls (12 to 16 pieces)

STEPS

———

1 **In a small bowl, make the vinegar water for dipping your hands by combining the water and 2 to 3 tablespoons (30 to 45 ml) of rice vinegar.**

2 **In a medium bowl, stir together the remaining 1 teaspoon (5 ml) rice vinegar, the sugar, and salt. Mix in the rice. Divide the rice into two portions.**

3 **Open a makisu (bamboo rolling mat) and place one sheet of nori on the mat, textured-side up. With wet hands, spread half the rice on the nori, leaving about one-fourth of the sheet uncovered along the top.**

4 **Apply a thin line of wasabi paste down the center of the rice and sprinkle some sesame seeds on top. Place half the tuna over the sesame seeds.**

5 **Roll your maki according to the "Basic Maki Technique" on page 106.**

6 **Repeat to make another roll. Cut each roll into 6 to 8 pieces. Serve with wasabi and soy sauce.**

This is one of the most basic rolls and it happens to be my daughter's favorite. I remember eating this as a healthy snack growing up. Kids can start learning how to make sushi with this roll, which can also be made with the nori on the inside (see "The Inside-Out Option," page 107) for those who prefer not to see it. You can replace the cucumber with takuan (sweet pickled relish).

Kappa Maki
Traditional Cucumber Roll

INGREDIENTS

——————

1 cup (240 ml) water

2 to 3 tablespoons plus 1 teaspoon (35 to 50 ml) rice vinegar

Heaping ½ teaspoon (2.5 g) sugar

Pinch sea salt

About 4 ounces (120 g) warm Steamed Japanese-Style Rice (page 71)

2 sheets nori

½ teaspoon (1.5 g) white sesame seeds

½ Japanese cucumber, peeled, halved lengthwise and again lengthwise to form 4 sticks

Wasabi powder mixed with water to form a paste, for serving

Soy sauce, for serving

Makes 2 rolls (12 to 16 pieces)

STEPS

——————

1 In a small bowl, make the vinegar water for dipping your hands by combining the water and 2 to 3 tablespoons (30 to 45 ml) of rice vinegar.

2 In a medium bowl, stir together the remaining 1 teaspoon (5 ml) rice vinegar, the sugar, and salt. Mix in the rice. Divide the rice into two portions.

3 Open a makisu (bamboo rolling mat) and place one nori sheet on it, textured-side up. With wet hands, evenly spread half the rice over the nori, leaving about one-fourth of the sheet uncovered along the top.

4 Apply a thin line of wasabi paste along the middle of the rice and sprinkle some sesame seeds on top. Place 2 cucumber sticks on the sesame seeds.

5 Roll your maki according to the "Basic Maki Technique" on page 106.

6 Repeat to make another roll. Cut each roll into 6 to 8 pieces and serve immediately with wasabi and soy sauce.

Hamachi is, of course, farm-raised yellowtail from Japan. It is almost buttery in texture, with a lovely bold flavor. This is my wife's favorite roll. You can replace the hamachi with any type of oily fish.

Negi Hama Maki
Traditional Hamachi and Scallion Roll

INGREDIENTS

———

1 cup (240 ml) water

2 to 3 tablespoons (30 to 45 ml) rice vinegar

2 to 2½ ounces (60 to 70 g) hamachi scraps, or fillets

2 scallions, trimmed to remove the last ½ inch (1 cm) of the root end, finely chopped

1 nori sheet

1 cup (200 g) freshly made Sushi Rice (page 72)

Soy sauce, for serving

Wasabi powder mixed with water to form a paste, for serving

Makes 1 roll (4 pieces)

STEPS

———

1 **In a small bowl, make the vinegar water for dipping your hands by combining the water and 2 to 3 tablespoons (30 to 45 ml) of rice vinegar.**

2 **In a small bowl, combine the hamachi and scallions.**

3 **Open a makisu (bamboo rolling mat) and place the nori sheet, textured-side up, on it. With wet hands, spread the sushi rice over three-fourths of the nori sheet, leaving about one-fourth of the sheet uncovered along the top. Spread the hamachi and scallions over the rice.**

4 **Roll your maki according to the "Basic Maki Technique" on page 106.**

5 **Cut the roll into 4 pieces. Serve immediately with soy sauce and wasabi.**

This is a pretty roll that is also healthy. A beautiful way to upcycle a variety of fish discards.

Rainbow Roll

INGREDIENTS

———

1 cup (240 ml) water

2 to 3 tablespoons (30 to 45 ml) rice vinegar

⅓ ounce (10 g) sashimi-grade tuna

⅓ ounce (10 g) sashimi-grade salmon

1 nori sheet, halved widthwise

1 cup (200 g) freshly made Sushi Rice (page 72)

1 avocado, pitted, peeled, and halved, then cut into ½-inch (1-cm) slices

1 Japanese cucumber, thinly sliced lengthwise into matchsticks

Soy sauce, for serving

Wasabi powder mixed with water to form a paste, for serving

Makes 2 rolls (8 pieces)

STEPS

———

1 In a small bowl, make the vinegar water for dipping your hands by combining the water and 2 to 3 tablespoons (30 to 45 ml) of rice vinegar.

2 Thinly slice the tuna and salmon at a sharp angle to maximize the size of the slices.

3 Open a makisu (bamboo rolling mat) and place a piece of plastic wrap, slightly larger than the nori sheet, on it. Place the half nori sheet on the plastic, textured-side up. With wet hands, thinly and evenly spread the sushi rice over the nori. Flip the nori so the rice is on the bottom (see "The Inside-Out Option," page 107).

4 Place half the avocado and cucumbers on the nori.

5 Roll your maki according to "The Inside-Out Option" on page 107. Keep the plastic wrap on.

6 Spread another sheet of plastic wrap on a cutting board and place half the tuna and half the salmon slices in an alternating pattern, somewhat overlapping, on the plastic. The goal is to have the roll look like a candy cane. Remove the plastic from the nori roll and place the roll on top of the fish. Roll tightly. Remove the plastic wrap.

7 Repeat with the remaining ingredients to make a second roll. Cut each roll into 4 pieces. Serve with soy sauce and wasabi.

This is a good entry roll for those new to sushi because no raw fish is used; instead, we used unagi kabayaki (grilled farmed freshwater eel). You buy the unagi grilled and frozen. I recommend looking for one that is 7 to 9 ounces (200 to 255 g) in size; larger ones tend to be chewy (the bigger the fish, the thicker the skin). If you're already a Dragon Roll expert, check out Chef Davin Waite's Master Variation and its accompanying photo at right.

Dragon Roll

INGREDIENTS

1 cup (240 ml) water

2 to 3 tablespoons (30 to 45 ml) rice vinegar

One 7- to 9-ounce (200 to 255 g) piece frozen unagi kabayaki, thawed

1 avocado, halved, pitted, and peeled

2 nori sheets, halved widthwise

1 cup (200 g) freshly made Sushi Rice (page 72)

½ Japanese cucumber, thinly sliced lengthwise into 8 to 10 pieces

White sesame seeds, toasted (optional), for garnishing

Unagi sauce, for serving (optional; see sidebar on page 116)

Makes 4 rolls (16 pieces)

STEPS

1 **In a small bowl, make the vinegar water for dipping your hands by combining the water and 2 to 3 tablespoons (30 to 45 ml) of rice vinegar.**

2 **Preheat the oven to 400°F (200°C).**

3 **Wrap the unagi in aluminum foil and place it in the oven for 3 to 5 minutes (for 7 ounces, or 200 g, to 9 ounces, or 255 g, respectively). Remove from the oven and slice the unagi into two long pieces (one for each roll).**

4 **Thinly slice each avocado half widthwise. With the side of the knife, gently press the avocado to fan out the slices.**

5 **Open a makisu (bamboo rolling mat) and place a piece of plastic wrap, slightly larger than the nori sheet, on it. Place one nori sheet on the plastic, textured-side up. With wet hands, thinly spread one-fourth of the sushi rice over the nori so you can still see it underneath. Flip the nori so the rice is on the bottom.**

6 **Place one-fourth of the cucumber slices and one piece of unagi on the nori.**

continued

For an upscale Dragon Roll, Chef Davin Waite rolled 2 pieces of shrimp tempura and 2 ounces (28 g) of crab inside a sheet of nori with 5 to 6 ounces (140 to 168 g) of rice applied to the outside. He topped the roll with 3 pieces of broiled eel (about 1½ ounces, 43 g, total; use anago or unagi) and 2 pieces of avocado. After covering the roll with plastic wrap and crimping with an uncovered makisu, he cut it into 8 pieces and topped it with eel sauce, tempura crunchies, masago, and scallions.

Dragon Roll *continued*

STEPS

7 Roll your maki according to "The Inside-Out Option" on page 107. Remove the plastic.

8 With the side of the knife, place 6 slices of fanned avocado on top of the roll. Using plastic wrap and the makisu, tightly roll the avocado slices around the nori.

9 Repeat with the remaining ingredients to make 3 more rolls. Cut each roll into 4 pieces, cutting through the plastic. Rinse your hocho (knife) after each cut to prevent losing the shape of the avocado.

10 Remove the plastic wrap and sprinkle toasted sesame seeds on the rolls (if using) or paint the rolls with unagi sauce as you like and serve.

MOST VALUABLE INGREDIENT

Do you know the one thing a sushi chef would rescue if their restaurant caught fire? The unagi sauce. While unagi sauce can be purchased, the traditional unagi sauces safeguarded by sushi chefs in Japan cannot be made overnight. Unagi sauce is made using an unagi's head and bones, mirin, sugar . . . the more ingredients, the better it tastes. And that's why they take it everywhere. Of course, store-bought unagi sauce isn't as pure as the real deal, but it works perfectly well for home chefs.

Awesome California Roll

CHEF KEN NAMBA | KIRIKO SUSHI |
Los Angeles, CA

The California roll is the first sushi created for Westerners. I remember having it in Roppongi, a district in Tokyo known for its nightlife, back in the 1980s. Sushi chefs in Los Angeles decided to substitute avocado for toro—a brilliant choice. Some sushi connoisseurs say the California roll is so basic they don't even eat it anymore. Their attitude is all wrong: I thought the same until then-famous Chef Toshi at Hama Sushi in Venice, California, made one for me and challenged me to see if he could break my naïve preconceptions. Oh my goodness! It was amazing. I asked him why it was so good. "Because I used real crabmeat, not the imitation crabmeat everyone else uses," he said. Fresh and real make the difference.

INGREDIENTS

1 cup (240 ml) water

2 to 3 tablespoons (30 to 45 ml) rice vinegar

1 nori sheet

1 cup (200 g) freshly made Sushi Rice (page 72)

1 medium avocado, peeled, pitted, and cut into 1-inch (2.5 cm) squares

10 ounces (280 g) chunk blue crabmeat

1 small Japanese cucumber, cut into matchsticks

Soy sauce, for serving

Wasabi powder mixed with water to form a paste, for serving

Makes 1 roll (4 to 6 pieces)

STEPS

1 **In a small bowl, make the vinegar water for dipping your hands by combining the water and 2 to 3 tablespoons (30 to 45 ml) of rice vinegar.**

2 **Open a makisu (bamboo rolling mat) and place a sheet of nori on it, textured-side up.**

3 **With wet hands, evenly spread the sushi rice over the nori, leaving about 1 inch (2.5 cm) at the top uncovered. Place the avocado and crabmeat in the center, and surround them with matchsticks.**

4 **Roll your maki according to the "Basic Maki Technique" on page 106.**

5 **Cut the roll into 4 to 6 pieces. Serve with soy sauce and wasabi.**

Note: This is a great roll to use "The Inside-Out Option" method of maki rolling. See page 107.

MASTER VARIATION
CHEFS YOYA TAKAHASHI AND MIKA MATSUI |
HAMASAKU | *Los Angeles, CA*

In the DJ Spider Roll, the chefs at Hamasaku make 6 crab cakes from 1 ounce (28 g) lobster tail (boiled while still in the shell) and 1 ounce (28 g) red crabmeat, blended with 1½ teaspoons of Japanese mayonnaise. They dollop each one with more Japanese mayonnaise and then bake the cakes at medium heat until the mayonnaise becomes golden.

Then they roll 2 slices of avocado and tempura flakes in soy paper covered with sushi rice (about 3 ounces, or 80 g, divided for 2 rolls). Thin slices of avocado are draped on top of the roll, which is then wrapped with plastic wrap and cut into 3 pieces per roll.

The pieces are laid flat and topped with one crab cake each, a drizzle of unagi sweet sauce, and tempura flakes.

Spider Roll

The best soft-shell crabs for this roll are fresh ones from Maine, when their fishery is open (usually spring to early summer). The second best choice is frozen soft-shells harvested in the United States. The frozen ones from Asia (Thailand, Malaysia) are good, but a little too meaty inside. However, they are less expensive than those from the United States. Prices also correlate to size—and the price goes up as the size increases (hotel, medium, large, jumbo, whale). The DJ Spider Roll pictured and featured in the Master Variation at left doesn't use soft-shell crab at all—it calls for red crabmeat.

INGREDIENTS

1 cup (240 ml) water

2 to 3 tablespoons (30 to 45 ml) rice vinegar

2 frozen medium soft-shell crabs

Oil, for pan-frying

1 teaspoon (5 ml) sriracha

1 tablespoon (15 g) mayonnaise

½ sheet nori, halved widthwise

3 cups (600 g) freshly made Sushi Rice (page 72)

4 bundles of 10 to 15 *kaiware* (daikon radish sprouts)

¼ avocado, peeled, pitted, and thinly sliced

Soy sauce, for serving

Wasabi powder mixed with water to form a paste, for serving

Makes 2 rolls (8 pieces)

STEPS

1 **In a small bowl, make the vinegar water for dipping your hands by combining the water and 2 to 3 tablespoons (30 to 45 ml) of rice vinegar.**

2 **Remove the frozen soft-shell crabs from the package. Coat the bottom of a skillet with oil and place it over medium-high heat. Add the crabs and fry until they turn light brown in color, about 4 minutes per side. Transfer to paper towels to drain.**

3 **While the crabs fry, mix together the sriracha and mayonnaise. Set aside.**

4 **Place one nori half sheet on a makisu (bamboo rolling mat), textured-side up. With wet hands, thinly spread half the sushi rice over the nori so you can still see it underneath, leaving about 1 inch (2.5 cm) at the top of the nori uncovered.**

5 **Place a crab, half the kaiware, and half the avocado on the rice. Sprinkle with half the sriracha mayonnaise. Roll your maki according to the "Basic Maki Technique" on page 106.**

6 **Repeat with the remaining ingredients to make another roll. Cut each roll into 4 pieces and serve with soy sauce and wasabi.**

Shrimp is a favorite for (almost) everyone in America and it makes a great introduction to sushi for those reluctant to eat raw fish. Using fresh shrimp is best, of course, but you can use frozen shrimp when you don't have time to prepare fresh shrimp or can't find any. And because the shrimp shrink when cooked, I recommend buying large ones.

Shrimp Tempura Roll

INGREDIENTS

4 large fresh or frozen shrimp, peeled and deveined

1 recipe Tempura (page 121)

1 cup (240 ml) water

2 to 3 tablespoons (30 to 45 ml) rice vinegar

1 cup (200 g) freshly made Sushi Rice (page 72)

1 nori sheet, halved widthwise

½ Japanese cucumber, thinly cut lengthwise into matchsticks

Soy sauce, for serving

Wasabi powder mixed with water to make a paste, for serving

Makes 4 pieces

STEPS

1 **Using a sharp knife, cut slits in the underside of the shrimp. This helps prevent curling while cooking.**

2 **Batter dip and fry the shrimp tempura style (see sidebar, page 121). Drain well.**

3 **In a small bowl, make the vinegar water for dipping your hands by combining the water and 2 to 3 tablespoons (30 to 45 ml) of rice vinegar.**

4 **Open a makisu (bamboo rolling mat) and place a piece of plastic wrap, slightly larger than the nori sheet, on it. With wet hands, thinly and evenly spread half the sushi rice on the plastic. Place one nori sheet on the rice, textured-side up.**

5 **Place 2 pieces of tempura in the center of the nori, leaving the tails of the shrimp hanging out so they won't be eaten.**

6 **Place half the cucumber on top.**

7 **Roll your maki according to "The Inside-Out Technique" on page 107. Keep the plastic wrap on.**

8 **Repeat with the remaining ingredients to make a second roll. Slice each roll into 2 pieces, cutting through the plastic. Remove the plastic wrap and serve immediately with soy sauce and wasabi.**

TEMPURA

Sometimes we fry seafood in a style called tempura. This deep-frying method is known for its beautiful flaky coating. The most common seafoods to use are shrimp and soft-shell crab, but you can also use this method on vegetables. Remember, tempura is about steaming the core of the fish or veggies while sealing the outside with batter. The inside will continue to cook for a couple of minutes after it's removed from the hot oil.

INGREDIENTS

Neutral cooking oil, for deep-frying

1 egg yolk

1 cup (240 ml) cold water

1 cup (106 g) pastry flour, plus more for coating

Shrimp, crab, or vegetables, as called for in the recipe

Makes 2 pieces

STEPS

1 In a deep skillet over medium-high heat, or in a deep-fryer, heat about 1 inch (2.5 cm) of oil to 350°F (180°C).

2 In a medium bowl, whisk the egg yolk and cold water. Add the flour to the egg mixture and whisk until just combined—the batter should be lumpy (see Tips).

3 Put some flour in a shallow bowl. Pat the fish or vegetables dry and, using your hands or chopsticks, coat it in the flour.

4 Dip the coated fish or vegetable in the tempura batter, covering it completely. Carefully slide the fish or vegetable into the hot oil. If the oil is hot enough, it will bubble furiously. Once the bubbles become smaller and the coating is lightly browned, transfer the tempura to paper towels to drain. Repeat with the remaining food.

Tips:

Keep the flour cold. Mix the batter over a bowl of ice water to keep it chilled.

Don't overmix the batter; leave lumps. We want tempura to be light and crispy.

Pat the fish or vegetables dry before coating with flour.

Don't fry too many pieces at once to prevent lowering the oil temperature.

I first encountered a spicy tuna roll when I moved to Los Angeles in 1989. Of course, it is not authentic sushi, but I remember it tasted good. This roll was born as a result of a sustainable mind-set. American consumers didn't want to eat tuna after it lost its red color, but chefs didn't want to throw away brown-colored tuna pieces (because they were still edible), so they started mixing it with something red (sriracha or chili paste). Customers liked it, and sushi bars reduced their fish waste—a win-win.

Spicy Tuna Roll

CHEF KEN NAMBA | KIRIKO SUSHI |
Los Angeles, CA

INGREDIENTS

1 cup (240 ml) water

2 to 3 tablespoons (30 to 45 ml) rice vinegar

½ (8 x 7-inch, or 20 x 18 cm) nori sheet

5 ounces (140 g) freshly made Sushi Rice (page 72)

1 heaping tablespoon (10 g) white sesame seeds, toasted

1 teaspoon (5 ml) sriracha

About 1½ ounces (40 g) sashimi-grade yellowfin, bigeye, or albacore tuna

3 avocado slices

½ Japanese cucumber, peeled and cut lengthwise into matchsticks

Soy sauce, for serving

Wasabi powder mixed with water to form a paste, for serving

Pickled ginger, for serving

Makes 1 roll (8 pieces)

STEPS

1 **In a small bowl, make the vinegar water for dipping your hands by combining the water and 2 to 3 tablespoons (30 to 45 ml) of rice vinegar.**

2 **Open a makisu (bamboo rolling mat) and place a piece of plastic wrap, slightly larger than the nori sheet, on it. Place the nori sheet on the plastic, textured-side up. With wet hands, evenly spread the sushi rice over the nori. Sprinkle the sesame seeds over the rice. Flip the nori so the rice is facing down.**

3 **Apply the sriracha in a single line across the center of the nori. Place the tuna, avocado, and cucumber on the sriracha.**

4 **Roll your maki according to "The Inside-Out Option" on page 107.**

5 **Cut the roll into 8 pieces, cutting through the plastic. Tighten the roll with the plastic wrap one last time. Remove the plastic wrap and serve with soy sauce, wasabi, and pickled ginger.**

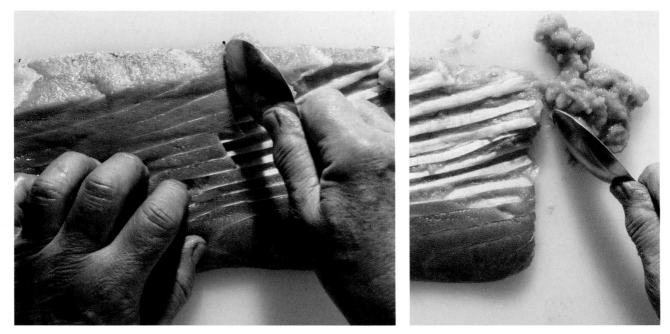

This is a good way to turn the expensive leftovers from making Tuna Nigiri (page 132) into a tasty finger food in minutes. This tastes great because the oil inside the toro will surface and the added shiso leaves, scallion, and takuan radish (pickled daikon) will cut the oiliness while adding subtle crunch. When preparing the shiso, scallions, and takuan, the finer you chop them, the finer the size and the smoother the flavor.

Crispy Toro Hand Roll

CHEF KEN NAMBA | KIRIKO SUSHI |
Los Angeles, CA

INGREDIENTS

1 cup (240 ml) water

2 to 3 tablespoons (30 to 45 ml) rice vinegar

10 ounces (280 g) bluefin or big-eye tuna's fatty portion (toro) scraps or trim, meat scraped off with a spoon, as needed

2 or 3 fresh shiso leaves, very finely minced

2 or 3 scallions, trimmed to remove the last ½ inch (1 cm) of white end, very finely minced

1 tablespoon (6 g) chopped takuan (yellow pickled daikon radish), very finely minced

About ¼ ounce (6 to 8 g) packaged crispy fried onions

1 nori sheet

Scant ⅓ cup (60 g) freshly made Sushi Rice (page 72)

Soy sauce, for serving

Wasabi powder mixed with water to form a paste, for serving

Makes 1 roll (4 to 6 pieces)

STEPS

1 **In a small bowl, make the vinegar water for dipping your hands by combining the water and 2 to 3 tablespoons (30 to 45 ml) of rice vinegar.**

2 **On a cutting board, combine the toro, shiso, scallions, takuan, and fried onions. Finely chop them all together.**

3 **Open a makisu (bamboo rolling mat) and place the nori on it, textured-side up. With wet hands, evenly spread the sushi rice over the nori, leaving a 1-inch (2.5 cm) border at the top uncovered. Place the chopped toro mixture in the center of the rice bed.**

4 **Roll your maki according to the "Basic Maki Technique" on page 106.**

5 **Cut the roll into 4 to 6 pieces. Serve with soy sauce and wasabi.**

Veggie Roll

CHEF DAVIN WAITE | WRENCH AND RODENT
SEABASSTROPUB | *San Diego, CA*

Vegetable sushi has been around in Japan for centuries. For the Japanese, fish and chicken were the only animal proteins until the late nineteenth century. The Japanese people used to consume (and still do) lots of vegetables, local to each area. Here we use cucumber, green bean, gobo (burdock), and avocado for a variety of textures and color. Feel free to pick and choose different vegetables to replace these if you prefer. For Chef Davin Waite's Master Variation pictured at right, called the BBQ Tuscan Kale Roll, check out the accompanying box. Veggie rolls are also a good gateway to sushi for those who don't like eating raw fish.

INGREDIENTS

1 cup (240 ml) water

2 to 3 tablespoons (30 to 45 ml) rice vinegar

1 nori sheet

¾ cup (150 g) freshly made Sushi Rice (page 72)

1 green bean

1 Japanese cucumber, cut into matchsticks

¼ avocado, peeled and chopped

Few *kaiware* (daikon radish) sprouts

One 8 x 1-inch (20 x 2.5 cm) piece *gobo* (burdock root), or fresh carrot, peeled

Soy sauce, for serving

Makes 8 pieces

STEPS

1 **In a small bowl, make the vinegar water for dipping your hands by combining the water and 2 to 3 tablespoons (30 to 45 ml) of rice vinegar.**

2 **Open a makisu (bamboo rolling mat) and place a piece of plastic wrap, slightly larger than the nori sheet, on it. Place the nori on the plastic, textured-side up. With wet hands, evenly spread the sushi rice over the nori. Flip the nori so the rice is on the bottom.**

3 **In a dry hot skillet, cook the green bean until lightly blackened around the edges. Chop.**

4 **Arrange the cucumber, avocado, green bean, radish sprouts, and gobo in a line across the middle of the nori.**

5 **Roll your maki according to "The Inside-Out Option" on page 107.**

6 **Cut the roll into 8 pieces, cutting through the plastic wrap. Tighten the roll with the plastic wrap one last time. Remove the plastic wrap and serve with soy sauce.**

MASTER VARIATION
CHEF DAVIN WAITE |
WRENCH AND RODENT SEABASSTROPUB |
San Diego, CA

For this BBQ Tuscan Kale Roll topped with Tuscan kale "kraut," Chef Davin uses a barbecue to grill one bunch of Tuscan kale drizzled with olive oil and seasoned with salt, pepper, and 2 teaspoons chopped garlic. Next, he sautes the kale and half an onion in some more olive oil until charred. He deglazes the pan with ½ cup (120 ml) sushi zu. Finally, he spreads 4 to 6 ounces (113 to 170 g) sushi rice over a piece of nori and flips it so the rice is on the outside, placing the BBQ kale, other leafy greens, and avocado inside, rolling it and then cutting it into 8 pieces. He tops the roll with the kale kraut and some sambal chile sauce for spice.

NIGIRI

———

Nigiri is a type of sushi consisting of a small rice ball topped with fish or another seafood with a dab of wasabi between. The basic method of making nigiri is always the same, but the fish preparation varies slightly for each fish type. Squid, for example, requires more subtle knife work because its flesh is firm compared to uni (sea urchin), whose flesh is creamy. The trick with uni is buying the right fish (see page 42). The same goes for buying unagi (eel; see page 42).

Squid with Hidden Knife Work, see sidebar on page 133

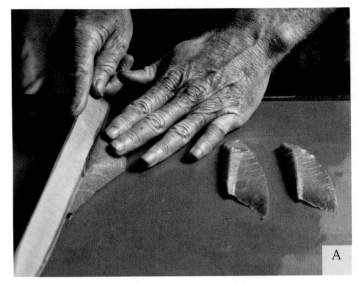

A

B

C

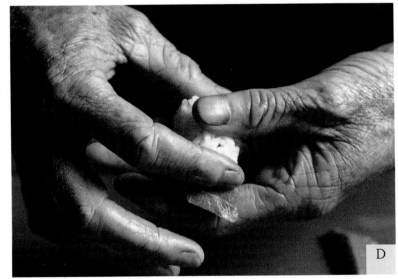

D

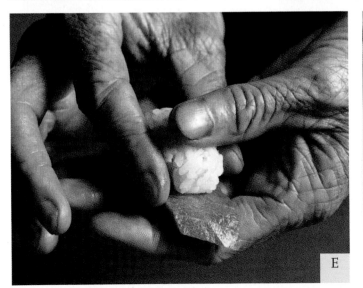

E

F

FORMING NIGIRI

A scant ¾ ounce (20 g) of sushi rice is an adequate amount for one piece of nigiri sushi. When forming nigiri, work with wet hands, so keep a bowl of vinegar water (1 cup, or 240 ml, water mixed with 3 tablespoons, or 45 ml, rice vinegar) handy.

01   On your right hand, wet your middle and ring fingers and wet the palm of your left hand.

02   With your right hand, pick up a scant ¾-ounce (20 g) portion of sushi rice and roughly shape it to the size of a Ping-Pong ball (don't worry about shaping it perfectly; you'll shape it again later).

03   While still holding the rice in your right hand, with your left thumb and index finger, pick up a piece of sliced tuna. As you open and turn over your left hand, let the tuna slice settle into the cup formed by your four fingers (not the thumb).

04   While holding the tuna in your left hand, pick up a small (pinky nail–size) portion of wasabi paste with the tip of your right index finger. Place the wasabi in the middle of the tuna slice.

05   Place the rice ball from your right hand onto the sushi over the wasabi. Push the middle of the rice ball softly, stretching the rice parallel to the long sides of the tuna slice (which is rectangular in shape). Use your left thumb to create a small indentation in the middle of the rice ball to make it an oval-ish rectangular shape. Now the rice ball has short and long sides.

ONE RICE BALL AT A TIME

When it comes to traditional nigiri, individuality rules. One rice ball is made at a time and immediately topped with a piece of sashimi and served before the rice gets cold. While making lots of rice balls at once is not the traditional method, for purchasing and preparation convenience, the recipes in this chapter are written for making more than one piece of nigiri at a time. Once you get accustomed to making the rice balls and placing the fish on top, I really encourage you to slow down the process and prepare and serve one piece of nigiri at a time.

06   Very gently, with your right thumb and right index finger, hold both short sides of the rice near the middle. With your right index finger, make an indentation parallel to the long side of the sliced tuna.

07   Let the entire thing (fish and rice ball; now you can call it nigiri) roll off your hand toward the left fingertips so the rice is now on the bottom and the tuna is on top.

08   Slide the nigiri about ¾ to 1 inch (2 to 2.5 cm) closer to the palm, still resting on your four fingers.

09   Using your right thumb and index finger, press the long sides inward to shape the nigiri.

10   While holding the short side of the nigiri with your left thumb, use your right index finger to press the nigiri down from the tuna slice to shape it.

11   With your right elbow out and away from your body, use your right fingers to turn the nigiri 180 degrees on your left palm.

12   Repeat steps 9 and 10. You have created the perfect nigiri!

A   *Slice the fish for nigiri. Tuna is pictured here.*

B   *Add some wasabi.*

C   *Next, add the rice.*

D   *Shape from the short side.*

E   *Shape from the long side.*

F   *Brush with Nikiri Sauce (page 159).*

The classic nigiri is a beautiful combination of red-colored tuna on white rice—the color contrast is what makes it look so appetizing.

After learning how to cut tuna into sashimi portions (see page 60), you can simply place the tuna sashimi pieces over sushi rice balls. You can also try making the rice balls smaller and rounder and the tuna pieces smaller. This, too, is a traditional form of sushi called temari sushi.

Tuna Nigiri

INGREDIENTS

---

1 cup (240 ml) water

2 to 3 tablespoons (30 to 45 ml) rice vinegar

Scant 1¼ cups (240 g) freshly made Sushi Rice (page 72)

Wasabi powder mixed with water to form a paste, for preparing the nigiri

14 ounces (395 g) sashimi-grade tuna, cut into sashimi portions (see page 60)

Soy sauce, for serving

Makes 12 pieces

STEPS

---

1 **In a small bowl, make the vinegar water for dipping your hands by combining the water and 2 to 3 tablespoons (30 to 45 ml) of rice vinegar.**

2 **With wet hands, form the sushi rice into 12 rice balls (scant ¾ ounce, or 20 g, each) as detailed on page 131.**

3 **Dab a little wasabi paste on each tuna portion and place one on top of each rice ball.**

4 **Serve immediately with soy sauce.**

Note: Please note that the flesh color of some tuna might be darker red, or red bean red, even though it is extremely fresh. Let me remind you again: Real tuna flesh doesn't have a florescent pink color. Tuna from Hawaii, Tahiti, Fiji, and Australia tend to have a brighter red color than tuna from Asia (Maldives, Indonesia, Philippines). The color of tuna flesh differs depending on where the tuna was harvested. Darker red doesn't mean it's not fresh.

HIDDEN KNIFE WORK

Kakushi bocho translates to "hidden knife work" in English and it can be very beneficial to making some fish's flesh a bit more palatable. Squid flesh, for example, is quite firm in contrast to the raw flesh of most fish. To mitigate this, Chef Ken Namba uses his *yanagi hocho* (knife) to add tiny slits to the squid flesh, as shown on page 129. This makes the squid easier to bite into and chew. And if you were to brush a sauce onto the tuna pictured here, the flavor of the sauce would be more easily transferred to the nigiri.

In this recipe, go light on the wasabi. Why? With white-fleshed fish, such as the fluke used here, you taste wasabi more than with oily fish, such as toro. This is because wasabi stimulates your senses through the nose rather than through the tongue. The oil from toro covers up the scent of wasabi, therefore you "taste" wasabi less than when you're eating a white fish such as fluke. Alternatively, you can replace the wasabi here with an even smaller amount of yuzu kosho (see page 53).

Fluke Nigiri

INGREDIENTS

―――――――

1 cup (240 ml) water

2 to 3 tablespoons (30 to 45 ml) rice vinegar

Scant 1¼ cups (240 g) freshly made Sushi Rice (page 72)

Wasabi powder mixed with water to form a paste, for making the nigiri

14 ounces (395 g) sashimi-grade fluke, cut into sashimi portions (see page 61)

Soy sauce, for serving

Makes 12 pieces

STEPS

―――――――

1 **In a small bowl, make the vinegar water for dipping your hands by combining the water and 2 to 3 tablespoons (30 to 45 ml) of rice vinegar.**

2 **With wet hands, form the sushi rice into 12 rice balls (scant ¾ ounce, or 20 g, each) as detailed on page 131.**

3 **Dab a bit of wasabi paste on each fish portion and place one on top of each rice ball.**

4 **Serve immediately with soy sauce.**

Many people think mackerel is visually unappealing and find its flavor too strong. However, if you can get fresh horse mackerel, it is quite different from what you might experience at a lower price point. A bonus is silver-skin fish has a higher nutritional value (EPA, DHA) than other fish. Small fish, such as aji, require a different process to cut sashimi pieces than bigger fish such as salmon and tuna. First, peel the aji skin off, then fillet it, take the pin bones out, and cut it against the grain.

Aji Nigiri
Horse Mackerel Nigiri

INGREDIENTS

1 cup (240 ml) water

2 to 3 tablespoons (30 to 45 ml) rice vinegar

Scant 1¼ cups (240 g) freshly made Sushi Rice (page 72)

Wasabi powder mixed with water to form a paste, for making the nigiri

14 ounces (395 g) sashimi-grade aji (horse mackerel), cut into sashimi portions (see headnote)

Grated peeled fresh ginger (*shoga*), for garnishing

Finely chopped scallion, for garnishing

Soy sauce, for serving

Makes 12 pieces

STEPS

1 **In a small bowl, make the vinegar water for dipping your hands by combining the water and 2 to 3 tablespoons (30 to 45 ml) of rice vinegar.**

2 **With wet hands, form the sushi rice into 12 rice balls (scant ¾ ounce, or 20 g, each) as detailed on page 131.**

3 **Dab a bit wasabi paste on each fish portion and place one on top of each rice ball.**

4 **Garnish each piece with a tiny bit of ginger and scallion. Serve immediately with soy sauce.**

Unagi (ranched freshwater eel) was not a traditional sushi item until about three decades ago. Anago (wild saltwater eel) had been used for authentic sushi. Even today, if you go to nicer sushi bars in Japan they don't have unagi, but always serve anago. Unagi is ranched, meaning the wild baby eels are caught and then grown to market size, and, as such, are sourced more easily than wild anago. Because it is ranched, it is much oilier than anago (ranched fish moves less than wild fish and, as a result, becomes oilier) and young Japanese seem to like it a lot—as much as Westerners.

Unagi Nigiri
Grilled Eel Nigiri

INGREDIENTS

One 8- to 9-ounce (225 to 255 g) piece frozen unagi kaba-yaki (grilled farmed freshwater eel), thawed

1 cup (240 ml) water

2 to 3 tablespoons (30 to 45 ml) rice vinegar

1 cup (200 g) freshly made Sushi Rice (page 72)

Wasabi powder mixed with water to form a paste, for making the nigiri

Unagi sauce (see Note, page 116), for glazing

Sansho, for serving

Makes 10 pieces

STEPS

1 **The unagi will be in an airtight package in a sauce. Open the package, remove the eel, and wipe off the sauce.**

2 **Make two cuts down the center of the fillet, one on either side of the spine. Remove and discard the spine. Holding your knife at a 45-degree angle, make long diagonal cuts about 1½ inches (3.5 cm) apart to cut the unagi into pieces for nigiri.**

3 **In a small bowl, make the vinegar water for dipping your hands by combining the water and 2 to 3 tablespoons (30 to 45 ml) of rice vinegar.**

4 **With wet hands, form the sushi rice into 10 balls (scant ¾ ounce, or 20 g, each) as detailed on page 131.**

5 **Dab a bit of wasabi paste on each eel portion and place one on top of each rice ball.**

6 **Brush each piece with the unagi sauce and sear with a kitchen torch until lightly charred. Alternatively, place under a preheated broiler just until lightly charred, watching it carefully.**

7 **Sprinkle each piece with sansho peppers (see page 49). Serve immediately.**

Ikura Nigiri
Salmon Roe Nigiri

Ikura is my kids' favorite seafood. They like the "pop" in their mouths and the saltiness. In recent years, the cost of good-size salmon roe has risen substantially. A pair of ikura nigiri at a restaurant used to be $4, but now it's between $7 and $8. So, I make my kids eat an ikura bowl (ikura over sushi rice) first to fill their bellies and then let them order ikura nigiri pieces.

We don't just use cured ikura like many inexpensive sushi bars that serve it as-is right from the package. You taste nothing but salty fish eggs in that case. We prep ikura so it tastes like high-end sushi bar ikura.

INGREDIENTS

¼ cup (60 ml) Dashi (page 153)

1 tablespoon (15 ml) soy sauce

1 tablespoon (15 ml) mirin, or sake if not serving to kids

4 ounces (115 g) cured ikura (salmon roe; make sure it's cured ikura, not raw)

1 cup (240 ml) water

2 to 3 tablespoons (30 to 45 ml) rice vinegar

1 cup (200 g) freshly made Sushi Rice (page 72)

4 nori sheets, cut lengthwise into 3 long strips

Wasabi powder mixed with water to form a paste, for making the nigiri

Nikiri Sauce (page 159), for brushing (optional)

Soy sauce, for brushing (optional) and serving

Makes 10 pieces

STEPS

1 In a medium bowl, stir together the dashi, soy sauce, and mirin. Add the ikura and stir gently to avoid breaking the eggs. Refrigerate for 20 to 30 minutes to cool the ikura and let it soak up the sauce. If you want to get the full flavor of the dashi and soy sauce, refrigerate for 1 day. The ikura will plump after soaking up the dashi and soy sauce.

2 In a small bowl, make the vinegar water for dipping your hands by combining the water and 2 to 3 tablespoons (30 to 45 ml) of rice vinegar. Set aside.

3 Drain the ikura through a fine-mesh sieve to remove the liquid.

4 To assemble the nigiri, with wet hands, form the sushi rice into 10 balls (scant ¾ ounce, or 20 g, each) as detailed on page 131. Wrap one nori strip around each rice ball. It should go around the rice ball about twice. Lightly wet the end and press it to seal.

5 Using a small spoon, place the ikura on the rice; one or two small spoonfuls is sufficient.

6 Place a dab of wasabi on top of the ikura.

7 Brush with nikiri sauce, or pour soy sauce over, to prevent dropping the topping into the soy sauce dish while trying to flip the ikura nigiri into the soy sauce. Serve immediately with soy sauce. You can also keep ikura, refrigerated in an airtight container, for up to 1 week.

Uni delivers an incredibly sweet flavor, but with an unusual texture that melts in your mouth. It is also often used in Italian pasta dishes.

Uni Nigiri
Sea Urchin Nigiri

INGREDIENTS

1 cup (240 ml) water

2 to 3 tablespoons (30 to 45 ml) rice vinegar

1 cup (200 g) freshly made Sushi Rice (page 72)

4 nori sheets, cut lengthwise into 3 long strips

3 ounces (85 g) prepared uni (see page 65)

Wasabi powder mixed with water to form a paste, for making the nigiri

Nikiri Sauce (page 159), for brushing (optional)

Soy sauce, for brushing (optional) and serving

Makes 10 pieces

STEPS

1 In a small bowl, make the vinegar water for dipping your hands by combining the water and 2 to 3 tablespoons (30 to 45 ml) of rice vinegar.

2 With wet hands, form the sushi rice into 10 balls (scant ¾ ounce, or 20 g, each) as detailed on page 131.

3 Wrap one nori strip around each rice ball. It should go around the rice ball about twice. Wet the end and press it to seal.

4 Using a small spoon, place two uni lobes on each nori-wrapped rice ball, gently folded so both ends are concealed.

5 Place a dab of wasabi on top of the uni.

6 Brush each with nikiri sauce, or pour soy sauce over, to prevent dropping the topping into the soy sauce dish while trying to flip the uni nigiri into the soy sauce. Serve immediately with soy sauce.

When I saw this for the first time, I thought it was some kind of tuna nigiri, and maybe the tuna had been marinated too long, or the marinade didn't have the right balance of ingredients—but, instead, it was made with a cube of aloe vera. Aloe vera has been known for years for its benefits to our skin and its detoxing effect. Many people use aloe juice in their smoothies. It can also be consumed as a vegetarian option for sushi. The skin has a bitter taste, so we remove that first.

Aloe Vera Cube Nigiri

INGREDIENTS

1 cup (240 ml) water

2 to 3 tablespoons (30 to 45 ml) rice vinegar

2 or 3 small raw beets

1½ to 2 ounces (45 to 55 g) fresh aloe vera, skin removed

Scant 1 cup (80 g) freshly made Sushi Rice (page 72), white or brown

Soy sauce, for serving

Wasabi powder mixed with water to form a paste, for serving

Makes 4 pieces

STEPS

1 **In a small bowl, make the vinegar water for dipping your hands by combining the water and 2 to 3 tablespoons (30 to 45 ml) of rice vinegar. Set aside.**

2 **Make beet juice by processing the beets in a high-speed blender or juicer. Strain the juice into a medium bowl and discard the solids. Set the juice aside.**

3 **Cut the skinned jelly portion of aloe vera into 4 pieces, about 1¼ x 2 inches (3 by 5 cm). Wash them with water to remove any sliminess. Add the aloe vera pieces to the beet juice and let sit for 30 minutes.**

4 **With wet hands, form the sushi rice into 4 rice balls (scant ¾ ounce, or 20 g, each) as detailed on page 131.**

5 **Place one piece of aloe vera on top of each rice ball. Serve immediately with soy sauce and wasabi.**

There are many sushi restaurants in Japan that offer vegetable sushi. Why not do it at your house, too? These recipes showcase the flavors, textures, and sweetness of the vegetables. You can use pretty much any vegetables that are in season (shun). You'll need 2 cups (400 g) freshly made Sushi Rice (page 72), divided, plus vinegar water for dipping your hands. And be sure to finish each one with a dash of soy sauce before serving.

Vegetable Sushi

CHEF HIROJI OBAYASHI | *Portland, OR*

RED BELL PEPPER SUSHI

1 red bell pepper

Pinch yuzu pepper paste

Makes 3 pieces

1 In a dry hot pan over high heat, cook the red pepper until the entire surface is charred. Peel and discard the skin; remove and discard the seeds. Cut the flesh into three pieces, about 1 inch (2.5 cm) wide.

2 With wet hands, form the sushi rice into 3 rice balls (scant ¾ ounce, or 20 g, each) as detailed on page 131.

3 Dab some yuzu pepper paste in the middle of a red pepper slice (watch out—yuzu pepper is spicy) and place the red pepper over a sushi rice ball, yuzu-side down. Repeat with the remaining pieces.

SHIITAKE SUSHI

1 large fresh shiitake mushroom, stem removed and discarded

1 teaspoon (5 ml) yuzu citrus juice

Makes 4 pieces

1 In a dry hot pan over high heat, cook the shiitake cap until you see moisture under the umbrella. Remove from the heat and cut into 4 pieces.

2 With wet hands, form the sushi rice into 4 rice balls (scant ¾ ounce, or 20 g, each) as detailed on page 131.

3 Place one shiitake piece over each rice ball.

4 Sprinkle with yuzu juice and serve.

EGGPLANT SUSHI

Olive oil, for cooking

1 Japanese eggplant, cut into 1 x 2-inch (2.5 x 5 cm) pieces

2-inch (5 cm) piece fresh ginger (*shoga*), peeled and grated

Makes 2 pieces

1 In a hot pan over medium heat, heat a sprinkling of olive oil. Add the eggplant and cook for 2 to 3 minutes until the eggplant softens slightly. You want a crisp surface, but tender inside.

2 With wet hands, form the sushi rice into 2 rice balls (scant ¾ ounce, or 20 g, each) as detailed on page 131.

3 Place one piece of eggplant over each rice ball.

4 Place some fresh ginger on the eggplant and serve immediately.

KING TRUMPET MUSHROOM SUSHI

1 teaspoon (5 ml) sesame oil

1 king trumpet mushroom

Pinch shichimi togarashi (see page 49)

Makes 1 piece

1 In a skillet over low heat, combine the sesame oil, king trumpet mushroom, and shichimi togarashi. Lightly sauté for 2 to 3 minutes until the mushroom loses its stiffness.

2 With wet hands, form the sushi rice into 1 rice ball (scant ¾ ounce, or 20 g, each) as detailed on page 131.

3 Place the mushroom on the rice ball and serve.

CAULIFLOWER SUSHI

2 cauliflower florets, thinly sliced

Grated fresh ginger (*shoga*)

Makes 2 pieces

1 In a dry hot pan over medium heat, cook the cauliflower until softened.

2 With wet hands, form the sushi rice into 2 rice balls (scant ¾ ounce, or 20 g, each) as detailed on page 131.

3 Place one cauliflower piece on each ball.

4 Top with grated ginger and serve.

SASHIMI

___

While nigiri contains rice and may contain raw fish, sashimi is thinly sliced raw meat—usually fish, such as salmon or tuna—served *without* rice.

Making sashimi looks easy. At sushi bars, chefs just slice the chunk of fish and place the slices on plates. It must be easy. They do it so fast and effortlessly, too. Well, go ahead and try. You'll end up with fish nuggets rather than thinly sliced sashimi. All fish is soft and somewhat fragile. So, you want to handle it as little as possible.

Knowing how to cut the fish, where to start cutting, and how to place the flesh on the cutting board all make a huge difference. Also, how you slice tuna (big fish) and fluke (small fish) are different—almost opposite. If you master cutting fluke, you'll be able to apply the technique on most other small fish—even shellfish and tentacles, if you want to explore.

When serving sashimi, plan to serve about 4 ounces (115 g) of fish per person. You can serve several kinds or only one kind. Each chef may garnish the plate slightly differently, but your typical garnish is thinly sliced cucumber, shiso leaves, pickled ginger slices, hair strings of daikon radish, and wasabi.

Tuna sashimi display

SOGI KIRI KNIFE TECHNIQUE

Sogi kiri is a technique used to thinly slice flesh on an angle so the slices are wider than when cut on a 90-degree angle to the cutting board. *Sogi* means "slice at an angle" in Japanese. The best type of fish for this is a lean white-fleshed fish, such as fluke, halibut, seabream, or flatfish, not an oily fish.

This slicing technique cuts vegetables and meat into slanted pieces to create more surface area so food soaks up more flavor from the ingredients, or cooks more quickly. It also makes a beautiful presentation and, when the sashimi pieces are cut to the perfect thickness, you enjoy the best flavor of the fish.

Place your saku (loin) on the cutting board with the thicker part on the right side, pointing slightly farther away from you than the left end of the saku.

Start slicing from the left side of the saku, holding the left end with your left middle and index fingers. Use your right hand to thinly slice the saku on an angle so the knife is almost parallel to the cutting surface; pull the hocho (knife) toward you, as if you're slicing the flesh right beneath your two left fingers. After each slice, use your left hand to stack the pieces.

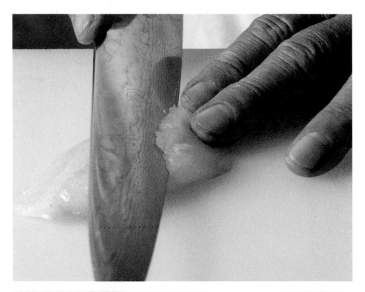

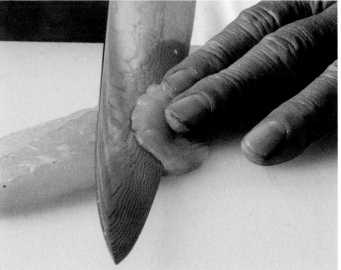

TUNA, FLUKE, AND SALMON SASHIMI

More in-depth instructions for cutting tuna, fluke, and salmon sashimi pieces are found on pages 58 to 64. Serve on plates with pickled ginger slices, thinly sliced cucumber, fresh daikon radish, shiso leaves, and wasabi.

Octopus is rarely sold fresh in U.S. markets, so if you want octopus for sashimi, look for cooked, frozen, and even sliced octopus. Some people avoid eating octopus because it's chewy. There are ways to make them tender even at this stage.

Octopus Sashimi

INGREDIENTS

1 octopus leg (weight varies)

Daikon radish, grated, or seltzer water, or houjicha tea

Soy sauce, for serving (optional)

Wasabi, for serving (optional)

Yuzu kosho, for serving (optional)

Extra-virgin olive oil, for serving (optional)

Sea salt, for serving (optional)

Nikiri Sauce, for brushing (page 159, optional)

Lemon wedges, for squeezing (optional)

Varies

STEPS

1 **Wearing kitchen gloves, massage the octopus with the grated daikon radish for 10 to 20 minutes.**

2 **Alternatively, in a small saucepan over high heat, combine the octopus with enough seltzer water to submerge it, bring to a boil, and boil for 2 to 3 minutes. Watch for the color to change to red and note that the texture should have some resilience. Drain and refrigerate.**

3 **Or, in a small saucepan over low heat, combine the octopus with houjicha tea, (houjicha is a traditional style of Japanese green tea made with bancha tea leaves from the autumn and winter harvests), and simmer for 10 minutes. Remove the octopus and let cool.**

4 **If you buy raw octopus, steam it to tenderize it. Boil some water in a steamer, drop the octopus into a steamer basket, and steam for 20 to 30 minutes over low heat. The water should evaporate.**

5 **Slice the octopus using the method for cutting fluke (see page 61).**

6 **Serve the sliced octopus with soy sauce and wasabi, or sprinkle with yuzu kosho, or extra-virgin olive oil and sea salt. Brush with nikiri sauce if you like your fish on the sweet side. A squeeze of lemon juice and a sprinkling of sea salt are nice, too.**

Aburi means "torching" in Japanese and it is done with a kitchen torch. It is a technique only applied to oily fish, to coax out more flavor and add a touch of sweetness. The goal is to sear the outside of the sashimi piece, leaving the inside raw. To enjoy this sushi at its best, eat immediately after searing. There are sushi bars in Japan where most of their sushi are aburi versions of familiar sushi fishes.

Aburi

CHEF DAVIN WAITE | WRENCH AND RODENT
SEABASSTROPUB | *San Diego, CA*

INGREDIENTS

7 ounces (200 g) Gindara brand farmed sablefish, cut as for sashimi (see page 144), at room temperature

Su-miso sauce (see Note), for garnishing

Edible flowers, for garnishing

Italian truffles, for garnishing

Scant 1¼ cups (240 g) freshly made Sushi Rice (page 72, optional, see Note)

Makes 6 pieces

STEPS

1 **Put the fish on a nonflammable surface, such as a disposable aluminum tray. Hold a kitchen torch about 6 inches (15 cm) away from the fish and apply the flame to the outside of the fish for only for a few seconds, sweeping the flame up and down.**

2 **Drizzle a line of su-miso sauce on the plate for each sushi piece, place one piece atop each, and serve garnished with the edible flowers and truffle shavings.**

Notes: To make su-miso sauce, stir together 2 parts white miso paste, 1 part rice vinegar, and 1 part sugar. You can also add wakarashi, Japanese hot mustard, to taste, for a bit of spiciness.

To make this dish nigiri, as pictured, make 6 rice balls and place a piece of sablefish on top of each one before torching.

SOUPS

Soup is served after sushi in Japan—which is opposite of how it is done in the Western world. Japanese soups tend to be healthful, healing, and simple to make.

The most widely known Japanese soup is made with miso, a paste made from fermented soybeans and barley or rice malt. It makes a robust and satisfying broth. There are also clear soups that can be sipped like a drink, but still have strong body. Many Japanese soups are made with dashi, a very simple broth that is a staple of Japanese cooking and made from just two ingredients—water and an ingredient of your choosing, such as kombu, bonito flakes, or shiitake mushrooms.

Of course, soup has a digestive benefit when you consume it with food. About four centuries ago, when sushi was a convenient fast food for construction workers in Tokyo, they were too busy to have soup before or after eating sushi. Instead, they washed down their sushi with giant cups of tea. Even today, if you go to sushi bars in Japan, they will serve hot green tea in a 10- or 12-ounce (300 to 360 ml) teacup. It feels almost odd, as everything else is so small.

Low-sodium versions of both red and white miso paste are widely available. If you like Japanese curry and rice and/or ramen noodles with curry-flavored broth, know that you can purchase curry-flavored miso paste.

White Miso Soup with Burdock Root

Gobo Miso Shiru

Obviously you can use many types or combinations of vegetables and meat in both white and red miso soups. One of my favorite vegetables to use is gobo, or burdock root. It is commonly enjoyed in Japan in miso soup and in salads (marinated in sesame oil) and infused into tea (zero caffeine). Rich in antioxidants and soluble fiber, it is said to help us retain warmth in our feet and hands in cold weather. Burdock root has a comfortable, earthy scent and is mild in flavor. I prefer not to peel the burdock root, as I like the roughness of the skin; however, if you'd like a more refined look, feel free to peel it in addition to slicing it.

INGREDIENTS

3½ cups (800 ml) water

6 inches (15 cm) gobo (burdock root), thinly cut into 1- to 2-inch (2.5 to 5 cm)-long matchsticks

3½ ounces (100 g) silk-screened or cotton-screened tofu, cut into ½-inch (1 cm) cubes

1 teaspoon (5 ml) Dashi (page 153)

3½ tablespoons (60 g) white miso paste

3 heaping tablespoons (20 g) finely chopped scallion, green part only

Pinch wakame (seaweed)

Serves 4

STEPS

1 **In a small saucepan over high heat, bring the water to a boil. Add the burdock root, tofu cubes, and dashi. Simmer for about 2 minutes until the burdock is tender.**

2 **Stir in the white miso paste, stirring until completely dissolved. Pour the soup into bowls and garnish with the scallion and wakame.**

Just like red wine, red miso soups work best with warm dishes. White miso soups pair well with warm dishes, too, but, personally, I feel having hot red miso soups in cold weather fills the bill. Nasu is Japanese for eggplant. You will see that red miso soup and purple eggplant blend well together, just like juicy steaks and dark red wine. By the way, the eggplant's skin is rich in antioxidants.

Red Miso Soup with Eggplant

Nasu Miso Shiru

INGREDIENTS

3½ to about 4½ ounces (100 to 125 g) Japanese eggplant

3⅓ cups (800 ml) water

4 teaspoons (20 ml) Dashi (page 153)

2½ heaping tablespoons (45 g) red miso paste

8-inch (20 cm) piece scallion, trimmed to remove the last ½ inch (1 cm) of the white end, thinly sliced

Serves 4

STEPS

1 **Cut the ends off the eggplant and halve the eggplant lengthwise. Place the long, flat side on your cutting board and cut the eggplant crosswise into half-moons about the width of your thumb.**

2 **In a small saucepan over high heat, bring the water to a boil. Add the dashi. Remove from the heat and stir in the red miso paste.**

3 **Add the eggplant to the pot and place it over medium heat. Cook for 2 to 3 minutes. Ladle into serving bowls and garnish with the scallion.**

Dashi

Dashi is an essential of Japanese cuisine. Because it is so well regarded as a flavor enhancer, even French chefs are eager to incorporate dashi into their cuisine. One reason for its popularity is dashi can swing both ways—it can make dishes saltier or sweeter, without adding sugar or salt. Naturally derived and healthy, dashi can be made from fish, meat, and vegetables.

INGREDIENTS

3⅓ cups (800 ml) water

⅓ ounce (10 g) dried kombu (seaweed)

About 2 heaping cups (20 g) *katsuobushi* (dried bonito flakes)

Makes about 3⅓ cups (800 ml)

STEPS

1   In a small saucepan over high heat, bring the water to a boil. When it starts to boil, remove it from the heat and add the kombu. Cover the pan and let soak for 15 minutes. That's it. If you keep the dashi on the heat after you throw in the kombu, the dashi will have a slimy texture.

2   Remove the kombu and add the katsuobushi. Let sit for 2 to 3 minutes. Strain the dashi through cheesecloth into a jar or bottle to filter out the katsuobushi. Cover and keep your homemade dashi refrigerated for 3 days, or freeze for up to 1 month.

Note: There are powdered, ready-to-use dashi packages available at American supermarkets today. However, these rip-and-ready packets are generally high in sodium (though there are low-sodium versions available) and with added preservatives to stabilize the quality for a longer shelf life. Instead, I would like you to make dashi from kombu, the same big dried sea kelp your kombucha tea is made from. You don't have to buy a $30 package of kombu; a $10 package is good enough for home cooking.

Ara means "discards" and jiru *means "soup" in Japanese. So, you can use the discards from your sushi prep in this soup. Soups are not only comforting, but they also have the added benefit of utilizing leftover fish or anything left from last night's dinner. This is a form of sustainability. While we work to reduce the amount of fish we catch from the oceans, we could certainly use more of each fish that we do catch so we need less fish from the ocean. Feel free to add any vegetables you like. Tofu is also good in this soup.*

Ara Jiru

INGREDIENTS

Sea salt

11 ounces (310 g) hamachi (Pacific yellowtail) discards

3 cups (720 ml) Dashi (page 153)

2-inch (5 cm) piece daikon radish, about 1½ inches (3.5 cm) in diameter, cubed

½ small carrot, diced

1-inch (2.5 cm) piece fresh ginger (*shoga*), peeled and grated

1 tablespoon (15 ml) cooking-grade sake

2 teaspoons (10 ml) mirin

1 teaspoon (6 g) red or white miso paste

2 or 3 scallions, trimmed to remove the last ½ inch (1 cm) of the white end

⅛ teaspoon shichimi togarashi (Japanese seven-spice blend)

Serves 4

STEPS

1 Sprinkle sea salt over the hamachi and then rinse thoroughly with warm water.

2 In a medium saucepan over medium-high heat, combine the dashi, daikon, carrot, and ginger. Bring to a boil and add the sake and mirin.

3 Reduce the heat to a simmer and add the hamachi. Continue to simmer until the hamachi is cooked through, 7 to 8 minutes.

4 Remove the soup from the heat and stir in the miso paste, stirring until dissolved.

5 Add the scallions and shichimi togarashi and serve.

Note: Be careful not to swallow the small bones!

Clear Broth with Tofu and Wakame

Miso soup with tofu and wakame is a very common menu item at sushi bars and other Japanese restaurants. Here we use dashi we make instead of miso to create a visibly light, yet comforting, soup. Of course, you can replace the tofu and wakame with other proteins and greens. My mother makes hers with grilled mochi instead of tofu every New Year—to this day, it is one of my favorite dishes that she makes! Just grill the mochi and add it to the clear broth. The mochi will start melting like fresh mozzarella cheese does in warm pasta sauce. The Japanese people like mochi because it is sticky—and sticks to your stomach. After eating mochi, you won't be hungry again for a long time....

INGREDIENTS

1 ounce (30 g) wakame (seaweed)

1½ to 1¾ cups (360 to 420 ml) Dashi (page 153)

4 ounces (115 g) silk or cotton tofu, diced

2 teaspoons (10 ml) soy sauce

Pinch sea salt

Serves 4

STEPS

1 Soak the dry wakame in 1 cup (240 ml) of room temperature water for 5 minutes. Squeeze the water from the wakame and place it on a paper towel to drain.

2 In a small saucepan over medium heat, combine the dashi and tofu. Bring to a boil. Remove from the heat and add the drained wakame and soy sauce.

3 Season with salt and serve.

Hot or cold, this hearty soup is delicious, but I prefer sipping cold corn soup to start a meal on warm summer days.

Corn Soup

CHEF HIROJI OBAYASHI | *Portland, OR*

INGREDIENTS

6 ears corn, in their husks

2 small potatoes

2 cups (480 ml) Dashi (page 153)

1½ to 1¾ cups (360 to 420 ml) Clear Broth (page 156)

½ cup (120 ml) heavy whipping cream

2 tablespoons (34 g) white miso paste

Pinch sea salt

Pinch ground white pepper

Serves 4

STEPS

1 **Bring a large pot of water to a boil over high heat. Add the corn, still in their husks, and the potatoes. Cook for 5 minutes, or until the potato is soft when poked. Drain well and let cool.**

2 **When the vegetables are cool enough to handle, remove the husks from the corn and cut the kernels off the cobs. Peel the potatoes.**

3 **In a clean pot over medium heat, combine the dashi, clear broth, and cream. Heat until warm.**

4 **In a food processor, combine the corn, potatoes, dashi mixture, miso paste, salt, and pepper. Purée until smooth. Pass the mixture through a fine-mesh sieve to filter out any solid pieces.**

5 **Serve hot in individual soup bowls or refrigerate for a couple of hours and serve cold.**

GARNISHES

––––––

There are several ways to garnish fish for
sashimi and nigiri. Use these guidelines to
replicate authentic applications.

LEMON SQUEEZE

This is commonly accompanied with sea salt on white-fleshed fish. Don't use too much—just a couple drops are enough. Then, sprinkle a pinch of sea salt over the fish. I recommend eating the fish immediately, as the citrus juice starts "cooking" the fish quickly and will change the texture and flavor.

SEA SALT

As mentioned previously, sea salt is used along with lemon juice. Some chefs prefer kosher salt over sea salt because it has no aftertaste. I enjoy thinking about salt in the same way a winemaker might think about "terroir." For example, I like to pair Hawaiian lava salt with Hawaiian tuna or Dead Sea salt with Mediterranean dorado.

YUZU KOSHO (YUZU PEPPER)

You can find *yuzu kosho* in paste form—usually in a small jar. It is spicy and citrusy with a subtle sweetness. A cotton swab–size portion is adequate for a piece of sashimi or nigiri fish. It also works nicely with white-fleshed fish, and I even use it when I grill chicken and pork chops.

GRATED GINGER

Fresh ginger (*shoga*) is often peeled and finely grated on a microplane. It is frequently served with ponzu sauce when preparing sashimi or sushi with silver-skinned fish, such as sardines or Spanish mackerel.

CHOPPED SCALLION

Chopped scallions are always an appropriate garnish. They go hand in hand with almost all garnishes listed here—especially on silver-skinned fish, along with ponzu sauce and grated ginger. Silver-skinned fish, typically, has soft, oily flesh; ponzu sauce and grated ginger cut the greasiness while the scallion adds texture.

Ponzu Sauce

Ponzu is a citrus-based sauce used in Japanese cuisine as a marinade or an addition to soy sauce. It is made by boiling rice wine, rice vinegar, dried bonito flakes, and seaweed and then straining and infusing with a Japanese citrus fruit, such as yuzu. When soy sauce is too assertive to allow the subtle flavors of white-fleshed fish, such as fluke and red snapper, to come through, citrusy ponzu sauce is a great alternative.

1 medium piece (⅓ ounce, or 10 g) kombu, wiped clean on both sides with a damp cloth

About 5 heaping cups (50 g) *katsuobushi* (dried bonito flakes)

1⅔ cups (400 ml) soy sauce

1¼ cups (300 ml) yuzu juice

10 to 12 tablespoons (150 to 180 ml) freshly squeezed orange juice

¼ cup (60 ml) rice vinegar

Makes about 4 cups (940 ml)

1 **In a medium glass bowl, stir together all the ingredients. Refrigerate for 3 days.**

2 **Strain the sauce through a cheesecloth into a 1-quart (960 ml) bottle. Cover and refrigerate for 3 to 4 weeks.**

Nikiri Sauce

This is what sushi chefs brush onto your nigiri sushi. To me, it has a more "rounded" flavor than store-bought soy sauce. It contains mirin, sake, and, sometimes, dashi, but I don't use it here because the dashi can overpower the delicate flavor of sushi if your nikiri doesn't come out perfectly. Each chef makes nikiri a little differently. Boil the soy sauce to eliminate any impurities and the alcohol.

10 tablespoons (150 ml) soy sauce

1 tablespoon (15 ml) sake

2 teaspoons (10 ml) mirin

Makes about ¾ cup (175 ml)

In a small saucepan over medium-high heat, combine the soy sauce, sake, and mirin. Bring to a boil and boil for 10 to 15 seconds. Remove from the heat. Let cool to room temperature, or refrigerate for faster cooling. Keep refrigerated in an airtight container for 2 to 3 days.

Sustainability
You Can Practice

Seafood consumption is on the rise globally. The world population is expected to grow. Will there be plenty of fish in the ocean in the future? Is tuna going extinct? Don't we need to consider protecting the incomes of fishermen as a part of sustainability, too?

While we cannot do everything right, there are things we can easily do that will have a positive impact on protecting our precious seafood resources. All the suggestions I make here are nothing but common sense.

———

Consume mature fish.

———

Eat fish in its shun *(peak season).*

———

Utilize as many parts of the fish as you can.

———

Enjoy a wide variety of fish.

———

Expect to pay fair prices for fair practices.

FARMED OR WILD?

For years I have been involved in the development of sustainable fisheries. The world's bluefin tuna stocks are heavily overfished, but you cannot overestimate the popularity of bluefin tuna with the Japanese people. When we look for alternatives, we have to think of the fishermen, simply supporting their families, but, at the same time, who are contributing to the depletion of the bluefin stock in the oceans.

Researchers at Kindai University in Japan have successfully started to raise Pacific bluefin tuna completely in captivity. I'm promoting their technology in other countries. It's easy to criticize bluefin tuna ranchers and fishermen, but it's not easy to provide a viable alternative.

I've also been supporting Tahiti's tuna fishery with business from the United States. The Moarii family has been leading the way in Tahiti to protect Tahitian fishing. I have been working with them since 2011. They were recently awarded for their sustainable farming practices by Marine Stewardship Council. This is rare for "longline" fishing, but I was not surprised because I know how passionate the family has been about protecting their local fishery and empowering the local community at the same time.

GINDARA FARMED SABLEFISH

Gindara Sablefish is the name of a sablefish farm located on the northern west coast of Canada's Vancouver Island. *Gindara* is the Japanese word for sablefish, also known as black cod. Most of the world's sablefish catch is from the icy Alaskan waters, from March through September. This species is prized for its delicate yet firm snow-white flesh, buttery flavor, and silky mouth-feel. And, unlike Atlantic cod or wild sablefish, this branded, farmed sablefish can be enjoyed as sushi and sashimi.

This unique fish farm is located in Kyuquot Sound, in a 300-foot (91.5 m) deep fjord. There, in the naturally cold oceanic environment where sablefish are found, Gindara farmed sablefish are raised from eggs without the use of antibiotics, hormones, or chemical treatments. The fish are confined in sea cages at a very low population density. This keeps the fish safe from predators and ensures a minimal effect on the environment. Gindara sablefish are raised under the guidelines of the Seafood Watch, Ocean Wise, and SeaChoice standards for the best choice in sustainability.

MY HASHI MOVEMENT

"My Hashi, My Heart" is a campaign to encourage people to carry their own chopsticks instead of using the free—environmentally unsound—*waribashi* (disposable chopsticks) provided at convenience stores and restaurants for one-time use.

Simply purchase your own hashi at stores or online and carry them when you go to restaurants.

GLOSSARY

ABURI Lightly grilled or torched fish topping on nigiri sushi.

AHI Yellowfin tuna.

AJI Spanish mackerel, also called horse mackerel.

ANAGO Wild saltwater eel.

ANKIMO Monkfish liver.

ARA JIRU Soup (*jiru*) made from fish scraps.

DASHI Japanese soup stock, usually made from seaweed and dried fish.

DEBA Japanese-style kitchen knife primarily used to cut fish.

FLUKE Type of flatfish.

GARI Pickled ginger; served with sushi as a palate cleanser.

GOBO Burdock root.

GOMA Sesame seeds.

GOMA-AE Both a sauce made of sesame seeds and a popular dish made of vegetables with a sesame dressing.

HAMACHI Japanese yellowtail or amberfish.

HASHI Chopsticks.

HOCHO Japanese word for "knife."

IZAKAYA A Japanese tavern.

KATSUO Bonito, a type of tuna.

KOCHUJANG A Korean sauce made from red chile peppers, rice, and fermented soybeans.

KOMBU A seaweed, also called kelp.

MAKI Rolled sushi.

MAKISU Bamboo rolling mat used to make maki.

MISO Fermented soybean paste.

MIZUNA Water greens.

NIGIRI A rice ball topped with fish.

NIKIRI SAUCE A glaze made from soy sauce, dashi, mirin, and sake brushed on sushi before serving.

NORI Thin sheets of seaweed that have been dried and toasted to enhance flavor.

OMAKASE Japanese phrase meaning, "I'll leave it up to you"; a meal made of dishes the chef selects for the customer.

ONIGIRI Rice balls with various types of stuffing.

O-TORO The most marbled parts of a bluefin tuna's belly.

POKE A Hawaiian dish of rice typically topped with cubed pieces of raw seafood, flavored with soy sauce and sesame oil, with added toppings such as edamame and sesame seeds.

SAKE Japanese for "salmon"; also a fermented rice wine.

SAKU A trimmed block of tuna ready to be cut for sushi or sashimi.

SANTOKU All-purpose Japanese knife with a wide blade.

SASHIMI Sliced or prepared raw fish.

SATOYAMA A sustainable-living foresting and farming community where people become part of the ecosystem, living near the border of the *sato*, village, and *yama*, or mountain.

SHAMOJI Large, flat, spoonlike utensil used for scooping rice.

SHISO An herb in the mint family; also called perilla leaves or ooba leaves.

SHOGA Ginger root.

SHUN Peak seasonality for fresh foods.

SINEW Tissue that ties muscle to bone.

SRIRACHA Condiment made of puréed chile peppers.

TAKUAN Pickled daikon radish.

TORO Fatty tuna.

TOSAZU A bonito-flavored dressing made from rice vinegar that is Japanese in origin.

TSUKEMONO Pickled vegetables.

UMAMI A fifth taste described as savory that naturally occurs in meats, vegetables, and dairy products.

UNAGI Freshwater eel.

UNI Sea urchin.

WAKAME Seaweed.

WAKARASHI Japanese hot mustard.

YANAGI Long slicing knife designed to cut thin slices of fish for sushi and sashimi.

ZUKE Method of preserving fish by soaking it in soy sauce.

RESOURCES

SEAFOOD AND JAPANESE FOODS

Chains

NIJIYA MARKET
www.nijiya.com

A small chain that features Japanese products and seafood, found in California and Hawaii.

MITSUWA MARKETPLACE
www.mitsuwa.com

A small chain that features Japanese products and seafood (at some locations). Stores are located in California, Hawaii, Illinois, New Jersey, and Texas.

HAN AH RHEUM/SUPER-H/H-MART
www.hmart.com

A rapidly expanding Korean supermarket chain with stores In California, Colorado, Illinois, Maryland, New Jersey, New York, Pennsylvania, Washington, and Washington, D.C.

WEGMANS
www.wegmans.com

Supermarket chain that sells sustainably sourced fish, with about 100 stores across the states of Maryland, Massachusetts, New Jersey, New York, Pennsylvania, and Virginia.

UWAJIMAYA
www.uwajimaya.com

A mini chain of Asian specialty supermarkets with four locations in the Seattle area, including Seattle, Bellevue, Renton, and Beaverton.

WHOLE FOODS
www.wholefoods.com

Supermarket chain that sells sustainably sourced seafood with stores throughout North America.

Trusted Wholesalers

The companies listed here are ones where I know you, the consumer, can call and be treated fairly. I have some other preferred wholesalers as well, but they are not set up for walk-in customers requesting smaller volumes.

CALIFORNIA
Los Angeles

Kanaloa Seafood
www.kanaloaseafood.com

King Fish
www.fishkingseafood.com

Santa Monica Seafood
www.smseafoodmarket.com

San Diego

Catalina Offshore Products
www.catalinaop.com

San Francisco

Osprey Seafood
www.ospreyseafood.com

COLORADO
Denver

Northeast Seafood Products
www.northeastseafood.com

MARYLAND
Elkridge

J.J. McDonnell
www.jjmcdonnell.com

HAWAII
Honolulu, Maui, Kauai, Kona

Garden & Valley Isle Seafood, Inc.
www.gvisfd.com

Individual Markets

ONE WORLD MARKET
www.oneworldmarket.us

42705-B Grand River Avenue
Novi, MI 48375

KATAGIRI JAPANESE GROCERY
http://katagiri.com

370 Lexington Avenue
New York, NY 10017

TENSUKE MARKET
Tensukemarket.com

1167 Old Henderson Road
Columbus, OH 43220

Online Only

CHOPSTICKS
www.cropsticks.co

Cropsticks: Onetime-use chopsticks made from fast-growing bamboo (instead of wood) with built-in rests.

Sustainability Certification Body

MARINE STEWARDSHIP COUNCIL
www.msc.org/what-you-can-do/buy-sustainable-seafood

CHEF CONTRIBUTORS

CHEF KEN NAMBA
Kiriko Sushi | Los Angeles, CA

Chef Ken Namba grew up in Tsukiji and understands delicacies. His restaurant, Kiriko Sushi, is known for delicious food that is consistently of the highest quality, and for its amazing service. Namba named the restaurant Kiriko after Edo Kiriko, a Japanese glass craft from Edo (present-day Tokyo) that involves cutting patterns onto the surface of glass, a practice cultivated among the townspeople during the Meiji period (mid-nineteenth century). The craft introduced Western influences while preserving traditional techniques. Ken envisions his restaurant will carry out the same philosophy.

Kiriko Sushi delivers an authentic taste of Japan with creative flair from the modern influences of sushi restaurants in Tokyo. Ken has been one of the big brothers of sushi chefs in the Los Angeles area for decades.

CHEFS YOYA TAKAHASHI AND MIKA MATSUI
Hamasaku | Los Angeles, CA

Hamasaku is one the best getaways for sushi connoisseurs to reach that next level. The chefs, Yoya Takahashi and Mika Matsui, both from Kyoto, understand the Westerner's palate and challenge them with authentic Japanese cooking. Sustainability is their foundation. They source uber-grade fish from Japan and the best handled local catches to support local fisheries.

CHEF MASA SASAKI
Sasaki | San Francisco, CA

After earning a Michelin star at Maruya in San Francisco, California, Chef Masa Sasaki left in pursuit of his own sushi restaurant, Sasaki. Only an omaske menu is offered. Sasaki emphasizes simplicity, focusing on traditional sushi and using intricate methods of smoking, curing, and marinating. He and his wife love motorcycles.

CHEF MASAYUKI FURUKAWA
Masa Sushi | Kumegawa, Tokyo, Japan

Before Chef Masa took over his restaurant from his father, he worked for the famous sushi chef, Keiji Nakazawa (Sushi Sho, Ritz Carlton Residence, Honolulu, Hawaii), whose disciples received numerous Michelin stars (though he refused them). He's the next generation of young Japanese sushi chefs who keeps tradition alive while updating his cuisine to the modern culinary arts. His anago is insane. I used to go there with my parents, and have been taking my kids there since they were little. So, his sushi restaurant connects three generations of my family.

CHEF HIROJI OBAYASHI
Retired | Portland, OR

Chef Obayashi moved to the United States from Tokyo in 1978. After working at Los Angeles's historical Imperial Gardens, he opened Hirozen Gourmet in 1989. His restaurant became a "best kept secret" among Hollywood's heavy hitters. He is a different breed of Japanese chef who can communicate with mainstream non-Japanese chefs in English. Hence, he taught many famous French chefs while he was consulting for the Four Seasons Hotel group. After he sold the restaurant, he and his wife, Yasuyo, moved to Portland, Oregon. He continues to consult internationally while offering Japanese cooking classes at his residence, just to share his knowledge with local people.

CHEF DAVIN WAITE
Wrench and Rodent Seabasstropub, The Whet Noodle | San Diego, CA

Davin Waite runs a hole-in-the-wall joint in San Diego irreverently named Wrench and Rodent Seabasstropub. His cult following flocks there for magical dishes such as swordfish bone marrow shots and yellowtail belly with chimichurri. At his adjacent restaurant, The Whet Noodle, customers line up for bowls of heart-warming ramen. Both eateries share a kitchen showcasing locally sourced produce and zero-waste practices.

Waite was taken under the wing of a Japanese chef while at college in Santa Barbara. He worked his way up from the bottom until opening the Fish Joint in 2004. Waite is known for whole-animal butchery and using whole foods without wasting anything. He believes great sushi is honest—with two or three ingredients, there is nothing to hide behind. It's all about the harmonious balance of what goes into each bite.

ABOUT THE AUTHOR

Nick Sakagami was born in Tokyo and owns his own seafood importing and consulting businesses. A longtime resident of Los Angeles, California, he is the only person outside of Japan to be certified as an *osakana meister*—or fish master. He can identify every sushi fish species and their subspecies by taste, feel, sight, and smell and he has an expertise in tuna. Sakagami believes he has a responsibility to share what he knows with consumers of seafood and the seafood industry.

After briefly working in the advertising industry, Nick started dealing with fish at a sashimi-grade seafood wholesaler in Los Angeles. He found the field to be very exciting and decided to expand his knowledge by traveling the world to learn more about fish. Today, Nick speaks with wholesalers about sustainable fishing and good import practices and influences high-end restaurants on buying practices.

Nick believes that sushi is part of the overall Japanese lifestyle and can be enjoyed most harmoniously when paired with sake and flowers (*Ikebana* style) to represent the current season. He is a certified sake advisor and is aiming to become a sake sommelier next.

ACKNOWLEDGMENTS

Thank you to the amazing team at Quarry Books: Jonathan Simcosky, Meredith Quinn, Anne Re, Mary Cassells, and Andrea Chesman. Thanks also to the photographers who helped make this book beautiful: Kristen Teig and Laia Albaladejo.

I am always in awe of the chefs who contributed to this book and who let me shoot photos in their restaurants: Chef Davin Waite (Wrench and Rodent Seabasstropub, Oceanside, CA); Chef Ken Namba (Kiriko, West Los Angeles, CA); Chef Masa Sasaki (Sasaki, San Francisco, CA); Chefs Yoya Takahashi, Mika Matsui, and Reimon Akabane (Hamasaku, Los Angeles, CA); Chef Hiroji Obayashi, who retired to Portland, OR; Chef Masayuki Furukawa (Masa Sushi, Kumegawa, Tokyo); and Chef Yuki Hanada (Sushi Hanada, Oxnard, CA), who taught me the vigor and rhythm of Edo-mae sushi.

I also am grateful to the Osakana Meister organization, which helped me get the permits needed to take photos in the legendary Tsukiji Fish Market.

And, last but certainly not least, thank you to my wife, Alison, who supported me with spending time for writing this book on many weekends.

INDEX